Michael Cramer

# Iron Cu...3

**Along ...        m
the German-Czech Border to the Black Sea**

An original *bikeline*-tour book

Esterbauer

Michael Cramer
*bikeline*®-tour book
**Iron Curtain Trail 3**
© 2010, **Verlag Esterbauer GmbH**
A-3751 Rodingersdorf, Hauptstr. 31
Tel.: +43/2983/28982-0, Fax: -500
E-Mail: bikeline@esterbauer.com
www.esterbauer.com
1st Edition 2010
**ISBN: 978-3-85000-279-0**

Please quote edition and ISBN number
in all correspondence!

Cover photo: Marco Bertram; Michael Cramer
Photo credits: Stefan Appelius: 144; Marco Bertram:
10, 11, 14, 17, 20, 23, 24, 28, 30, 32, 34, 36, 37,
38, 40, 44, 49, 50, 53, 56, 63, 65, 66, 68, 73, 75,
78, 80, 82, 88, 90, 94, 98, 100, 105, 106, 108,
110, 112, 114, 116, 118, 119, 120, 122, 124, 125,
126, 127, 128, 130, 132, 134, 136, 138, 140, 142,
145, 146, 148, 150, 152, 154, 155, 156, 158, 160,
161, 162, 164, 166, 168, 170, 172, 174, 176, 178,
179; Michael Cramer: 6, 8, 19, 70, 72, 74, 76, 81;
Roland Esterbauer: 60; Michael Manowada: 54; Gaby
Sipöcz: 45;

**We wish to thank all the people who contributed
to the production of this book.**
The cycline-Team: Heidi Authried, Beatrix Bauer, Markus Belz, Michael Bernhard, Michael Binder, Veronika Bock, Karin Brunner, Sandra Eisner, Roland Esterbauer, Angela Frischauf, Gabi Glasstetter, Melanie Grubmüller, Dagmar Güldenpfennig, Carmen Hager, Heidi Huber, Martina Kreindl, Eveline Müllauer, Gregor Münch, Karin Neichsner, Niki Nowak, Julia Pelikan, Petra Riss, Christian Schlechte, Erik Schmidt, Matthias Thal, Martin Wischin, Wolfgang Zangerl.

# bikeline

**What is bikeline?**

We are a team of writers, cartographers, geographers and other staff united by our enthusiasm for bicycling and touring. Our project first "got rolling" in 1987, when a group of Vienna cyclists came together to begin producing bicycling maps. Today we are a highly successful publisher that offers a wide range of bikeline® and cycline® books in five languages covering many European countries.

We need your help to keep our books up-to-date. Please write to us if you find errors or changes. We would also be grateful for experiences and impressions from your own cycling tours.

We look forward to your letters and emails (redaktion@esterbauer.com),

Your bikeline team

# Preface

Taking you through a tangible part of European history - that is the goal of the Iron Curtain Trail. It winds its way through vestiges of the cold war across Europe, from the Barents Sea to the Black Sea. The route not only connects European culture, history and sustainable tourism, but guides the interested cyclist through a diversity of landscapes and the unique biotopes of the European Green Belt that were able to establish themselves in the no man's land between East and West.

This third volume documents the southern section of the Trail, from the German-Czech border at Hof to the Bulgarian-Turkish border by the Black Sea at Carevo, about 3300 km away. The route takes the cyclist over the heights of the Bohemian Forest, past Moravia and the Slovak capital Bratislava and on to cross the Danube River at Vienna. Along the southern border of Hungary the route goes through Slovenia and Croatia and then mostly follows the Danube River between Romania and Serbia before reaching Bulgaria. The last part of the route then follows the Bulgarian borders with the former Yugoslav Republic of Macedonia, Greece and Turkey, before ending at the Bulgarian Black Sea coast.

With route descriptions and packed with maps, historical background information and tips on cultural highlights and attractions in each region, as well as practical information on travel and accommodation, this guide is an invaluable companion on the journey of discovery along the former Iron Curtain.

3

**map legend**

## Cycle route

**Main cycle route, low motor traffic**
- —— paved road
- – – – unpaved road
- ······· bad surface

**Cycle path / main cycle route, without motor traffic**
- —— paved road
- – – – unpaved road
- ······· bad surface

**Excursion or alternative route, low motor traffic**
- —— paved road
- – – – unpaved road
- ······· bad surface

**Excursion or alternative route, without motor traffic /cycle path**
- —— paved road
- – – – unpaved road
- ······· bad surface

- —— other cycle routes
- ooooooo planned cycle path
- xxxxxx closed cycle path
- ooooo ferry connection

## Vehicular traffic

- •••••• cycle route with moderate motor traffic
- ▪▪▪▪▪▪ cycle route with heavy motor traffic
- ▪▪▪▪▪▪ cycle lane
- —— road with moderate motor traffic
- —— road with heavy motor traffic

## In city maps

- 🅿 parking lot*
- 🅟 garage*
- ✉ post office*
- 🅰 pharmacy*
- 🄷 hospital*
- 🅵 fire-brigade*
- Ⓤ police*
- 🦉 theatre*

## Topographic informationen

- ⊖ international border
- country border
- forest
- ········· embankment, dyke
- Staumauer (dam, groyne
- Autobahn (motorway
- Hauptstraße (main road
- secondary main road
- minor road
- carriageway
- ▭ railway
- narrow gage railway
- ～500～ contour line

**Maßstab 1 : 300.000**

1 cm ≙ 3 km

| 0 | 5 | 10 | 15 | 20 | 25 | 30 | 35 | 40 | 45 | 50 | 55 | 60 km |

# Contents

## The Author

Michael Cramer was born on June 16th, 1949 in Gevelsberg in Westphalia and attended the Reichenbach Lycée in Ennepetal. From 1969 to 1974 he studied music, physical education and teaching in Mainz. From 1975 until 1995 he was a teacher at the Ernst-Abbé-Lycée and at the Albrecht-Dürer-Lycée in Berlin-Neukölln.

From 1989 until 2004 Michael Cramer was the transportation expert for The Greens caucus in the Berlin city parliament and from 1989 until 1990 chairman of the committee on transportation and municipal services. Simultaneously he taught several courses at the Otto-Suhr-Institute of the Berlin Free University in order to teach students about transportation policies for the city. He has published widely in his field.

Cramer is motivated in his interest in German-German history by three events from his youth:

In 1961, when the Berlin Wall was erected, he had his first vacation without his parents to the fishing village of St. Peter Ording on the North Sea coast. Not only did he stare at the beach sailors, but he also listened to the tales of the legendary Count Luckner, about whom it was related that he could, with his bare hands, tear up telephone books and bend five-mark coins.

One day the newspapers blared with headlines about "Wall in Berlin built – will there be a Third World War? He remembered the stories of his parents about the war, and was terribly frightened that he too might have to live through such a terrible time.

Two years later he travelled to West Berlin for the first time – this was as a soccer player in his local team, TuS Ennepetal – a trip many sport clubs, organisations, church congregations made; in Berlin his team played against BFC Südring. For the first time he ate a curry sausage – at the time not to be had in West Germany – and played

www.michael-cramer.eu

for the first time miniature golf in the Hasenheide park – something he also couldn't do in Ennepetal, and he also had his first taste of Fassbrause (Apple-flavored soda, something not available in West-Germany today). His aunt had presented him with a camera and he took his first pictures – of the Berlin Wall in the Bernauer Straße.

From then on, every time he came to Berlin he came to the Bernauer Straße and observed how the wall changed. At the beginning, the windows on the ground floor and the floor above it were sealed, later the buildings were demolished, with the exception of the facade of the ground floor, finally this was also demolished and followed by a 'modern' wall.

Shortly after he read his first political book: "The Revolution dismisses its children", by Wolfgang Leonhardt, who, as the child of communist parents had to flee Nazi-Germany for the Soviet Union. Shortly after their arrival in the Soviet Union, Leonhardt's mother was arrested and deported to Siberia. Her son Wolfgang was put in orphanages and educated to be a socialist. As a committed Communist he belonged to the 'Ulbricht Group' which was sent to Germany when the Soviet Union occupied Germany at the end of the war, the job was to establish a working German administration. After he managed to get his mother released from her labour camp in 1948 and the doubts about his loyalty began to grow, he fled East Germany in 1949 and went to Yugoslavia, which at the time felt itself not as a member of the East Bloc.

After completing his studies in Mainz in 1974, Michael Cramer moved to Berlin (West) as a convinced 'Germany-Politician', where he confirmed an old adage: "either you pack up and leave after six months, or you stay forever in Berlin".

During the summer of 1989 he first biked around the Berlin Wall, 100 miles, the 'customs path' around West-Berlin. It was virtually impossible to get lost: all one had to do was ride alongside the wall. In the autumn, the Wall fell; he was able to repeat his tour, this time on the 'border guard path' between the inner and outer Wall. This was the moment he had the idea of a Berlin Wall Trail.

It took, however, 10 years before the idea could become a reality. The reason: after the fall of the Wall, the motto all over was 'The Wall must go!' – and, true to their training – Prussian, Socialist, thorough – the border troops of the former GDR took down by October 2nd, 1990. Only in cases where the local district authorities, organizations or individuals prevented them from being extra thorough was it possible to leave parts of the Wall standing.

On the occasion of the 40th anniversary of the building of the Wall (August 13th, 2001), Cramer once again started working on his idea. He conceived of Wall tours during the summer of 2001 and was able to convince the city government and the Berlin parliament to place the rest of the Wall on the list of protected landmarks; signs were put up along the path and the path itself was re-paved to be bicycle-friendly.

In 2001 Michael Cramer's book "Berlin Wall Trail" appeared, a guide book to the 100 mile long route along the former Berlin Wall; it has been revised several times and it also appeared in 2003 in an English edition. In 2004 Cramer published the guide "San Francisco Bay Trail", about the 450 mile long bicycle trailaround San Francisco Bay.

The "German-German Border Trail" first appeared in the summer of 2007 and presented by Wolfgang Thierse, Vice President of the German Bundestag, as the German section of the European 'Iron Curtain Trail' at the Europe House in Berlin. During the presentation Thierse quoted former Commission President Jacques Delors: "The European Union is like a bicycle: if you stop it, it falls over!"

Since 1979 Michael Cramer has been living in Berlin without a car: he uses his bicycle, buses, local trains and taxis and when on vacation he prefers the soft tourism. For those reasons he not only knows the situation in and around Berlin, but has learned biking routes in the United States, Switzerland, Austria, France and Germany literally 'by the seat of his pants'.

Since 2004 Michael Cramer is a member of the Greens in the European Parliament

# Introduction

Experiencing history. This book cannot be described in a shorter or better way. It describes a cycling tour, which was totally unimaginable two decades ago. It starts at the Barents Sea on the border between Finland and Russia and runs along the former Iron Curtain through Mid-Europe to the border between Bulgaria and Turkey on the Black Sea. What a contrast! Where two world systems were once armed to the teeth against each other, cycle tourists from around the world can and should experience Europe together. This is something the people could only dream about up to 1989 and which became reality twenty years ago through the peaceful revolution in Eastern Mid-Europe. Those who follow the cycle trail – naturally in stages – will be continuously confronted with the 20th century history of Europe. In many locations, the traces of the Iron Curtain are merely visible to experts. Therefore, small and large monuments can be often found which tell of the – often tragic – history of the time during the European division. No cyclist will remain untouched by these historical landmarks.

The present cycle tour book is the vision of an enthusiast which was brought to paper, one who turned an idea into reality with friendly and inexhaustible perseverance: As a member of the Greens in the Berlin House of Representatives, Michael Cramer had committed himself to the marking and development of a cycle trail along the former wall around West Berlin while the politicians and administration still aspired to remove every trace of this border. When he reached his target in Berlin with the "Berlin Wall Trail", he dedicated himself to the development of an inner German cycling trail which he documented with his second cycling tour book, the "German German Border Trail". The path to this target was hardly levelled when Cramer, as member of the European Parliament, focused his dedication on the European level. Thereby it was not only his target to document the "Iron Curtain Trail" in the present cycle tour book. He was also successful in his efforts

**Rainer Eppelmann**

of acquiring funding from the EU for the development of cycle tourism in Eastern Mid-Europe.

Just in time for the 20th anniversary of the peaceful revolution, the well-documented Iron Curtain Trail is a symbol of the freedom that the people peacefully fought for in Eastern Mid-Europe in 1989. Could it be any nicer to explore the past than in a casual manner during the nicest time of the year, during vacation? The Federal Foundation for Reconciliation of the SED Dictatorship is happy to be able to make a small contribution to the present tour book. In their name, cyclists who are preparing themselves for their tour through Europe are wished suitable weather, a problem free journey and many interesting impressions.

Rainer Eppelmann

Chairman of the Federation for the Reconciliation of the SED Dictatorship

# Iron Curtain Trail

The Iron Curtain stretched over a distance of almost 7,000 kilometres through Europe from the Barents Sea to the Black Sea and divided the continent into east and west. Until the peaceful revolutions in Eastern and Mid-Europe, it was the physical and ideological border between two hostile blocs. Not only were many neighbouring countries separated thereby, but also Germany was divided into east and west. Today there is hardly anything left to see of the former death strip, the remnants are no longer a dividing line.

Memories however must be made visible! We know that there are no mutual memories between west and east. The eastern and western Europeans have very different memories of the border, also because it was interpreted completely contrarily by the official politics in both parts of Europe. What the Warsaw Pact countries glorified as "protection from the class enemy", was seen by the western countries as a symbol of the lack of freedom that socialism actually provided.

Visible memories are already present with the "Berlin Wall Trail". For the 40th anniversary of the erection of the wall, I initiated a proposal, as a member of the Berlin House of Representatives, in which the senate was requested to designate a cycle and hiking trail along the former border, to place the remaining portions of the wall under monument conservation, to design it cycle-friendly and to signpost it. The public is invited to the "wall forays" by the Alliance '90/The Greens which have been performed every summer by the author since the year 2001. The book "Berlin Wall Trail" was simultaneously published by the Esterbauer Verlag in the series *bikeline*, in which the 160 kilometres around West Berlin – 40 kilometres between the two city halves, 120 kilometres between West Berlin and the surrounding – were described.

After the proposal was accepted in the Berlin House of Representatives, the senate dedicated themselves to the realization of the wall trail. Since then the trail has been signposted and developed cycle and hiker friendly. A memorial was erected for the last victim of the wall, Chris Gueffroy. Nearly all remaining authentic relicts have been placed under monument conservation in the meantime.

As an addition to the marking of the former course of the wall and the artistic design of the border crossings, the "Berlin Wall History Mile" was brought to life. It is a permanent exhibition in four languages (German, English, French, and Russian), with information about the history of the division, construction and opening of the wall at over 30 locations. Photos and short texts describe the events which took place at the respective locations. The "Berlin Wall Trail" became part of Berlin's tourism programme and is the first project which combines "soft" tourism with city tourism. One can actually "experience" the history, culture and politics in Berlin in its true sense.

9

Not only Berlin, but also Germany was divided for several decades. It is also important to remember the 1,400 kilometres long inner German border. Therefore the national caucuses of the SPD and the Alliance '90/The Greens submitted a proposal to the German Parliament (DS 15/3454) on June 30, 2004 to transform the former death strip into a living space. It would be developed for "soft tourism" and be a part of a European Green Belt along the former "Iron Curtain". The German Parliament voted unanimously in favour thereof in December 2004.

The "German-German Border Trail" along the "Green Belt" leads along 150 nature preservation areas and integrates numerous flora-fauna habitat areas, the three biosphere reservations Schaalsee, Elbaue and Rhön as well as the national park Harz. It leads from the Baltic Sea to the Czech border along numerous rivers and lakes and takes you over the Harz Mountains as well as through the forests of Thuringia. It passes many memorials and border land

museums as well as some still remaining observation towers.

Europe was also divided for many decades. The Iron Curtain stretched from the Barents Sea on the Norwegian-Russian border to the Black Sea. Today it is no longer a divider. It is a symbol of a common and total European experience in a reunited Europe. This was also a reason why a large majority of the European Parliament voted for the proposal of the author to create the Iron Curtain Trail in his report on "New Perspectives and Challenges for a sustainable European Tourism". It is a part of the

collective memory with which the often invoked European identity can be promoted.

The history of the division of Europe did not begin with the end of World War II, but rather when Hitler seized power on January 30, 1933 and when German troops marched into Poland at the beginning of the World War II on September 1, 1939. Without the triggering of World War II by Nazi Germany, Europe would not have been divided.

The anti-Hitler coalition, despite its differing ideologies, was united in the common fight against National Socialist Germany. Things changed, however, shortly after the German army's unconditional surrender. On March 5, 1946, the former British Prime Minister Winston Churchill, who had been voted out of office after the end of the war, stated in his famous speech in Fulton, Missouri that part of Europe had disappeared behind an "Iron Curtain", creating a division of Europe. The Cold War had begun.

Since the leaders of the Warsaw Pact States were not willing to grant political freedom and proved incapable of solving their countries' economic problems, there were repeated uprisings. The popular uprising in the GDR on June 17, 1953 was the first in the Soviet-controlled bloc after World War II. It was followed in 1956 by the Poznań demonstrations in June and the Hungarian Revolution in October, the Prague Spring in 1968, the Charter 77 in Czechoslovakia as well as the birth of the Solidarność movement in Poland in 1980. The activities of the Solidarność trade union, Hungary's success in reaching out to the West, the independence movements in the Baltic states and the removal of the barbed wire fence at the Hungarian-Austrian border by the two countries' Foreign Ministers Gyula Horn and Alois Mock on June 27, 1989 all paved the way for the fall of the Iron Curtain on 9 November 1989 and thus the end of the Iron Curtain in Europe.

Using the Berlin Wall Trail and the German German Border Trail as examples, a cycle and hiking trail is to be developed along the previous Iron Curtain on the former death strip,

which allows travels along the common history of our continent. Since 2002, the 6,800 kilometre long "Green Belt" from the Barents Sea to the Black Sea has been under the patronage of Mikhail Gorbachev, the former President of the Soviet Union and now President of "Green Cross International" (GCI). With this, the meaning of the Green Belt for the protection of nature and the value as symbol of the reunification of east and west is also internationally recognized. If the member states realize the project in collaboration with the European

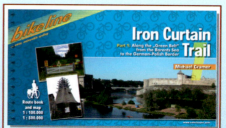

**Iron Curtain Trail 1**
Along the „Green Belt" from the Barents Sea to the German-Polish Border
1 : 75.000, 1 : 100.000, 1 : 400.000
**ISBN:** 978-3-85000-278-3

**Iron Curtain Trail 2**
Along the „Green Belt" from Usedom via the German-German Border Trail to the Czech Border
1 : 75.000, **ISBN:** 978-3-85000-279-0

Parliament and the EU Commission, one will also be able to experience European history, politics and culture.

Twenty countries, 14 thereof EU Member States, are involved in this project. The trail begins at the Barents Sea and follows the Norwegian-Russian border and the Finnish-Russian border to the Baltic Sea before heading along the coastline of Estonia, Latvia, Lithuania, Kaliningrad, Poland and the former GDR. From the Priwall Peninsula by Travemünde it follows the former border between East and West Germany to the point where Saxony, Bavaria and the Czech Republic meet. Then it follows the highlands of the Bohemian Forest, passes Moravia and the Slovak capital of Bratislava and crosses the Danube near Vienna. It then follows the southern border of Hungary via Slovenia and Croatia. Between Rumania and Serbia it mainly takes you along the Danube, through Bulgaria, the former Yugoslav Republic of Macedonia and Greece, to end at the most northern point of Turkey on the Bulgarian coast of the Black Sea.

The trail stretches over numerous national parks with interesting flora and fauna and combines a number of unique landscapes which have mostly remained untouched due to their vicinity to the border and former exclusion zones. It also connects countless monuments, museums and open-air facilities which commemorate the history of the division of Europe and the overcome with the peaceful revolutions in Eastern Mid-Europe.

As with the "Berlin Wall Trail" and the "German German Border Trail" the Iron Curtain Trail may use any of the paved border patrol roads that still exist. The project is being worked on in many countries and regions of Europe, and numerous sections have already been completed and signposted.

There are naturally many alternatives of which routes to take with the bike in the Green Belt. Whether on the western or eastern side, whether closer to the border or further away, or on perforated slab patrol roads or asphalt. The proposed route was selected based on the following five criteria:

- as close as possible to the former border
- on paths that are comfortable to ride on
- avoid high traffic streets
- often cross the former border
- integrate many sites that bear witness to history

The proposed route is to be understood as "work in progress". The local people naturally know more about their area, there are

# 1393 km

also always changes due to construction etc. Therefore, the author and the publisher are thankful for comments and suggestions which are based on the above mentioned criteria.

These three volumes of the "Iron Curtain Trail" would not have been possible without the support of other persons and institutions. Therefore I would like to greatly thank the "Foundation for the Reconciliation of the SED Dictatorship" for their generous support, who opened their archive and provided many historical photos.

I would also like to thank Roland Esterbauer and his colleagues for supporting the project from the beginning and for the professional realisation.

Since I – unlike in the books "Berlin Wall Trail" and "German German Border Trail" – was unable to cycle and describe the trail myself, I would especially like to thank the European friends who took over the compilation and description of the trail:

For volume 1 of the "Iron Curtain Trail", Timo Setälä cycled along the Norwegian-Russian and the Finnish-Russian section, followed by Frank Wurft who documented the Estonian-

Latvian part to Tallinn. My thanks go out to Stephan Felsberg for the portion from Tallinn via Lithuania, Kaliningrad and Poland to the German-Polish border.

For volume 2, the section from the German-Polish border to the Priwall Peninsula by Travemünde could be taken from the "Baltic Sea Trail 2" from the Esterbauer publishers. The section from the Baltic Sea to the German-Czech border was a revision of the "German-German Border Trail" which was published in 2007.

Pavel Svoboda was on the road for volume 3 along the Czech-German border.

Then Dr. Pavel Sroubek took over and documented the Slovakian-Austrian part of the route. Adam Bodor was responsible for the border stretch of Hungary with Austria, Slovenia, Croatia and Serbia. My thanks also go out to Marco Bertram for the final portion through Romania and Bulgaria with detours to Serbia, Macedonia, Greece and Turkey to the end of the cycle trail at the Black Sea.

I was greatly supported in the coordination of the project and the editing of the three books by Korbinian Frenzel, Christoph Gelbhaar, Uwe Giese, Antje Kapek, Jens Müller, Liesa Siedentopp and Erdmute Safranski who also receive my special thanks.

Further I would also like to thank the European initiative European Green Belt (www.greenbelt.eu), who brought the "Green Belt" project to life together with nature conservationists from the middle and eastern European countries, which in the mean time has become one of the most successful and symbolic European projects.

And finally I would like to thank Mikhail Gorbachev, who has been President of Green Cross International since 1993 and supported the project "Green Belt" with enthusiasm.

Twenty years have passed since the fall of the Iron Curtain in Europe. We know: only those who know their past will master the future. We all want to create a positive future, we all want to remember the decades of the division of our continent with wistfulness and with thanks to the overcome thereof, with the peaceful revolutions in Eastern Mid-Europe.

In this sense, I wish you good reading and great pleasure experiencing European history, politics and culture.

Michael Cramer

# About this book

This book contains all the information required for a cycling tour along the Iron Curtain Trail: maps, route description, accommodation options and the most important practical information and sights.

## The maps

The detailed maps are at a scale of 1 : 300.000. Apart from the exact route, the maps also provide information on the nature of the surface (sealed or unsealed), gradients (light or strong) and distances as well as cultural, touristic and gastronomic facilities along the route.

However, even the most accurate maps cannot replace looking at the written route description. Please note that the recommended main route is always indicated in red and purple, with variants and detours in orange. The exact significance of the individual symbols is given in the legend on page 4 and 5.

## The text

The text generally consists of a route description which the recommended main route follows.

Texts in orange describe variants to the main route or excursions to places of interest.

All important **places** are also given in bold type for greater ease of use.

Descriptions of individual places of historic, political, cultural or natural interest along the route also contribute to a worthwile travel experience. These blocks of text are printed in italics to distinguish them from the route description.

Texts in mauve indicate places where you must make a choice on your next section, interesting sights or leisure activities a little off the main route.

# From the border triangle to Aigen (A)                    383 km

### From the former border triangle to Cheb (Eger)      45 km

You can push the bike over the field along the signposted border triangle by Hinterprex and Oberzech, about 12 kilometres east of Hof. You will reach a small bridge over a stream on the Czech side of the border and a picnic site with several signposts. The surroundings of Hranice and Aš form a western tip of the Czech Republic, and here you will find a further tip in a miniaturised form: Over a distance of 1,500 metres, the Czech Republic is only 200 to 500 metres wide in this area. Turn right on the 20 kilometre long Iron Curtain Greenway, a compact trail towards the town of Aš. After a few kilometres, starting at the branch towards Hranice, the trail is paved and signposted as cycle trail 2058. Unfortunately, there are also numerous potholes – you are on the former border control road.

## The history of the Czech Republic

*The Czech Republic was formed on January 1, 1993 as a successor state of Czechoslova-*

*The author at the Dreiländereck*

*kia. The national territory basically comprised the former so-called "Bohemian Crown Lands" of Bohemia, Moravia and Moravia-Silesia.*

In the 9th century, Bohemia was divided between various Slavic tribes. Charlemagne attempted to seize the area several times, however with little success. After the collapse of the Great Moravian Empire, Bohemia voluntarily subdued to the king of East Francia, Arnulf of Carinthia. It however maintained a special position in the Holy Roman Empire, which was expressed on the hereditary Bohemian royal dignity – especially under the rule of the Premyslid Dynasty. After the approximately 400 year duration of the Premyslid Dynasty, Charles IV, King of Bohemia, was crowned Holy Roman Emperor in 1355. Prague was his residence. Between 1471 and 1526, the Bohemian crown was in the possession of the Polish Jagiellonian Dynasty. Since the Bohemian population elected Ferdinand I from the House of Habsburg to King of Bohemia in 1526, it subsequently belonged to Habsburg territory. Differences in confession and efforts towards autonomy provoked the Thirty Year War (1618-1648) which resulted in the following of the Protestants. After the end of the 18th century, the Czech national pride found new interest. Until 1918, the area remained in the reigning territory of the House of Habsburg.

*After World War I, the so-called First Republic of Czechoslovakia was created in 1918. In the Munich Agreement, the areas with a majority of German population (Sudetenland) were assigned to the German Empire in 1938.*

The southern portion of Slovakia and the Carpathian Ruthenia were assigned to Hungary, the Teschen area was occupied by Poland. Despite attempts to disarm Hitler-Germany, the German troops occupied the so-called "remaining Czechia" and placed them under German administration as Protectorate of Bohemia and Moravia. The massacre of the Reichs Wehrmacht in the villages of Lidice and Ležáky and the concentration camp on Czech territory showed the brutal treatment of the followed Jews, political opponents and minorities. US American, Soviet and Czechoslovakian troops freed the country in May 1945.

After the end of the war in 1945, the Czechoslovakian Republic (SR) regained its borders from 1918, except for Carpathian Ruthenia which fell to the Soviet Union. The SR, since 1960 the Czechoslovakian Socialist Republic (SSR), was a member of the Warsaw Pact and the Council for mutual economic aid in the influential area of the Soviet Union on the other side of the Iron Curtain. The "Prague Spring" in 1968 under Alexander Dubeck was an attempt at "Socialism with a

**Castle in Libá**

human face". He was defeated by the military intervention of the Warsaw Pact and a targeted government was implemented.

The resistance was however only temporarily broken: A civil rights movement named "Charta 77" led by the author Václav Havel continued to oppose the regime. When Michael Gorbachev reduced the pressure with his politics of Glasnost and Perestroyka, the resistance expanded to protests of many days. The "Velvet Revolution" forced the communist government to resign. Václav Havel was elected first president of the Czech and Slovak Federal Republic (SFR) which

existed from April 1990 to the end of 1992. The negotiations of January 1, 1993 between the Minister President of the Slovak Constituent Republic, Vladimír Meiar, and Václav Klaus, who had won the election in the Czech territory, led to the division of Czechoslovakia into two independent states – the Czech and Slovak Republics.

The Czech Republic became a member of NATO in 1999 and a member of the European Union on May 1, 2004.

Even less can be seen of the former community of Újezd (Mähring), which was in the middle of a clearing three kilometres to the southwest. Merely the war memorial erected in 1994 indicates the former population of this most western location of the Czech Republic. The train station Štítary, which you reach in the southeast, was once one of four districts (Ängerlein) of the destructed village of Schildern. From here, follow the little road to the right and you will come to Aš (Asch) via Krásná.

## Aš (Asch)

The tall and slender Neo Renaissance City Hall appears unproportional. Originally it was **19** closely surrounded by the houses of the old town, which were destroyed and finally torn down during the destruction of the war and the extensive depopulation due to expulsion and the erection of the border zone. It is now an eye-catcher in a park-like surrounding. The village marketplace in front of it can hardly be recognised and the once prominent Evangelic church of Holy Trinity behind it must be sought for. The Asch area was allowed to maintain its protestant religion after the Thirty Year War. However, the church built in 1622 was renovated in the architectural style of the Catholic Church, Baroque. After a fire in 1960, only the outer walls remained which were later torn down. The remaining walls are high enough to mark the foundation.

150 metres to the southeast, by the St. Nicholas' Church, you will find the city museum in a former castle of the family Zedtwitz. On the Háj (Hainberg) you will find one of the three towers of Bismarck maintained in the Czech Republic, from which you can enjoy a wide view of the Fichtel-, Elster- and Erz mountains.

Cheb

Leave the town to the south via the main road (**Chebská**). Continue straight towards the forester's house where the road is connected with the street 64 by a roundabout near Nový Žár. Pass a barrier and cross the railroad tracks on a newly constructed bridge and continue to the left. After several hundred metres you will once again reach the former convoy road of the border troops where you turn left. On the cycle trail 2063 and the Iron Curtain Greenway, you will encounter deteriorated pavement which you should watch out for. Furthermore there are stretches which are very steep.

After about five kilometres, turn left into the road 2066 to Libá (Liebenstein).

## Libá (Liebenstein)

The rococo castle, which the Zedtwitzer built to replace the destroyed castle, was completely ruined by the use of the army. A private investor is attempting to renovate the large construction, however has developed serious financial difficulties in the mean time.

If you leave the town to the south, you will travel along an idyllic lake and reach the original route again after two kilometres without making a detour. Here, where the former village of **Dubina** (Eichelberg) once was, you have a nice view over the valley of Ohře (Eger) and the Bavarian town of Hohenberg, which is on the other side of the valley across from the well maintained castle. Here the convoy road consists of concrete slabs and leads steep uphill to the rather venturesome looking old steel bridge over the Ohře. Continue through meadows and fields towards the border crossing Pomezí nad Ohí/Schirnding, where you will be directed under the E 48 on to the street

606. This leads to Pomezí nad Ohí along the shores of the Skalka reservoir. The cycle trail 2243 accompanies it to Cheb (Eger).

## Cheb (Eger)

The town with a population of 35,000 has the German name of the river. The Czech name originally means "bend". It originated at the foot of a castle, which was built in 1120 for the administration of the Bavarian Nordmark on the foundation of a 200 year older Slavic construction. The starting point for tour is the long triangular market place with its two fountains, in the middle of which Roland and Hercules stand guard. Across from the latter you will find the tourist information centre. The elaborate baroque, though unfinished, City Hall stimulates the visitor's interest as well as the Egerer Stöckl (palíek), a group of eleven Jewish merchant houses, which survived the city fire in the 13th century.

Behind that you will find the Pachelbel house, in which the all too powerful Prince Waldstein – called Wallenstein by Schiller – was murdered. It now houses the Museum of Local History which, apart from memorabilia of the military leader, shows an exhibition about 20 villages near the Egerland border, which were deserted and destroyed after 1945.

In the middle of 2008, the Gothic church of St. Nicholas once again received its steeple tops once again, which now crown the chancel side of the view from the market place. 300 metres to the west you will find the castle on the shores of the river, which Emperor Friedrich Barbarossa had built before it fell to the Bohemian King. The black tower, which is built from lava rocks, optically stands out. A particular highlight for architecture fans is the well maintained Roman double chapel. It was originally accessible from the ground floor and upper level of the palace. The ground floor was for the general population and

the upper level for the nobility, who were able to participate in church service through an octagonal opening in the ceiling.

Trains depart from the local station directly to Marktredwitz and Prague.

## From Cheb to Bärnau                                        27,96 ml

Due to the numerous one-way streets, it is not easy to return to the road 606 from the centre of town while obeying traffic rules. From the castle, continue south on **Dobrovského/Hradební**, turn left by a prominent multi-story building in the **Americká** and then right to the crossing in which the 214 (17. listopadu) merges on the opposite side. The highly travelled stretch leads past numerous petrol stations, restaurants and the shanty market – an absolute must – before you reach a memorial and then the no longer occupied border crossing Svatý Kříž (Heiligenkreuz)/Waldsassen.

## Memorial for the victims of the Iron Curtain

This memorial from Antonin Kaspar was inaugurated on June 27, 2006 together with the first Czech Foreign Minister after the fall of the wall, Jiří Dienstbier. It is dedicated to the people who lost their lives in an attempt to cross the border. The main thought is the broken chains. The memorial shows a list with the names of 82 people that lost their lives in the years from 1948 to 1981 at the western border. During the inauguration on the 56th anniversary of the execution of the politician Milada Horáková, about 20 people demonstrated, mainly former staff of the border regime.

## Milada Horáková

The lawyer and politician who actively opposed the Nazis during World War II was imprisoned for several years. After the war, she represented a political pluralism and was a delegate for the party of the Czechoslovakian National Socialists in Parliament. After the communists came to power in February 1948, she resigned in protest.

In a nine-month trial, Milada Horáková was sentenced to death. She was the only woman who was executed for political reasons on June 27, 1950 in the communist Czechoslovakia. The decision was revoked in 1968, but she was not rehabilitated until 1990. She is commemorated today by a memorial stone in Prague at the National Cemetery Vyšehrad.

## Svatý Kříž

Those coming from Cheb will find Waldsassen less interesting. For centuries it only included a cloister until the first houses were built in the 17th century.

The Iron Curtain Trail leaves the main road to the left by Hundsbach, where it leads to the left again to the 2175 via **Schloppach** and **Hatzenreuth**. Continue to the left towards Neualbenreuth via **Querenbach** and **Maiersreuth**.

## Neualbenreuth

The attractive town is characterised by a nice market square with timbered houses in the Egerland style. The Turmstraße leads to a borderland tower in about 2 kilometres distance, which was built by the territorial association of the Sudetenland in 1961 and became a landmark of the town.

The route leads to the south through an open landscape to **Altmugl**, where the stump of a giant beech tree with a circumference of 7.70 metres gives you an idea of the size of the tree, the top of which had to be cut in 1999. The next four kilometres continue through the forest. After two kilometres, the Czech border is rather close to the street.

*On the left you will find the small* **Church of St. Nicholas** *of the village of Högelstein which has been vacant since the Hussite Wars. Although the current construction is only about 100 years old, it is very striking due to the enchanted location.*

In **Mähring** turn left from the Hauptstraße into the **Treppensteiner Straße**. After 500 metres it runs into the east-west connection road 2167 where you turn right, and after 80 metres again left.

A narrow paved strip leads to **Treppenstein**, a former "Hammerherren" castle which is now contained in a large game reserve. The neighbouring trout farm offers great meals. The forest and gravel road continues close to the Czech border.

*A large erected stone commemorates Hans Dick, who was shot be the Czech border troops on German territory on September 18, 1986.*

Pass the road to Redenbach and continue on the forest trail until you have the possibility to continue to **Griesbach**. Here you will meet the 2172 which you follow to the left. From the village of **Asch**, continue slightly downhill through the forest area and after the button factory in **Beierfeld** over meadows and fields until you reach Bärnau.

## Bärnau

*The village of Bärnau, which belongs to the cloister Waldsassen, was expanded to a town in the middle of the 14th century. It has been a part of Bavaria since 1628 and could have been considered "structurally weak" already in the*

*Borderland tower by Neualbenreuth*

19th century. Only factories and light industry were considered for this area, which meant the production of buttons for Bärnau. Not less than 70 companies produced mother-of-pearl buttons at the peak of the development. There was even a "button school" and an international convention. They were, however, not able to keep up with the cost effective plastic and die casting buttons of the competitors and thus there are now only a few button factories left. In the German Button Museum you can still get an insight into the glorious days of the past, exhibitions of various materials and especially the processing of nacre.

The cosy village is worth visiting. If you can manage without electricity and running water, you should plan to spend the night in the borderland tower during the summer. It can be

**23**

found at an elevation of 800 metres south of the small border crossing and you can visit the Steinbergkirche on the left of the street.

## From Bärnau to Eslarn                    38 km

A small road leads through the fields to the more southern town of **Naab**, where you follow the orange-red-orange markings on the right after the silver cabin. Somewhat bumpy and curvy, but with very beautiful scenery, the route leads you through forests and past lonely wooden cabins. By the **silver cabin**, the centre of a well known cross country ski area, you will run into the Hauptstraße 2154 to Flossenbürg.

**Tip:** Although the route turns before you reach the village, it is worth a visit due to the topographic and historical reasons. From the tower you will have a magnificent view of the bizarre castle ruins. You will also find a lesson about the human cruelty and irreverence at the former concentration camp.

## Concentration camp Flossenbürg

Without any secrecy, the National Socialists had built a camp to which people mainly from

*Concentration Camp memorial site Flossenbürg*

the occupied areas in Eastern Europe were deported to. In the stone quarry they had to break granite for Hitler's monumental constructions on the mountain. The armour production began in 1943, in particular for the aircraft company Messerschmitt. Between 1938 and 1945, approximately 100,000 people were held captive in the concentration camp Flossenbürg and in more than 80 auxiliary camps, where up to 1,000 slept in one barrack which was meant for 300 prisoners. The resistance fighter Dietrich Bonhoeffer was executed here shortly before the end of the war and is commemorated with a memorial. A

total of 30,000 prisoners died, either through work, starvation or the freezing cold. The death march to Dachau shortly before the end of the war left a trail of more than 5,000 bodies on the side of the road.

After the release, a residential community was built on the premises of the camp, which is very similar to the arrangement of the barracks. Various parts of the camp are also used for commercial purposes. In June 2006, the remaining NS constructions and the quarry were declared a monument. One year later, after two generations, the first permanent exhibition was created: Concentration Camp Flossenbürg, Gedächtnisallee 5-7, open daily 9:00 to 17:00, admission free. www.gedenkstaette-flossenbuerg.de

The reputed NS criminal John Demjanjuk (*1920) was in numerous concentration camps and also warden in Flossenbürg as of October 1943. His duty number 1393 was the same that he was listed under in the Sobibor Extermination Camp. After World War II he left Germany and emigrated to the USA. From there he was transferred to Israel in 1986 where he was sentenced to death for the crimes in the extermination camp Treblinka. In 1993 the decision was revoked and he returned to the USA.

In May 2009, Demjanjuk was transferred from the USA to Germany and has been in pre-trial custody since then. On July 13, 2009, he was accused of accessory to murder in at least 27,900 cases by the Prosecutor's Office Munich I. John Demjanjuk is the last living war criminal who must answer before the court.

Before Flossenbürg, the "Green Roof Cycle Trail" continues slightly uphill to the east. It continues through a forestry area to Waldkirch.

From here continue on the 2154 towards **Gehenhammer**, an old hammer and sawmill at an elevation of 664 metres which also houses a small mull museum with an old fashioned sandwich shop. Continue slightly downhill towards **Krautwinkel** and from there

then left uphill to **Neukirchen** zu St. Christoph with its unusual church tower that is turned by 45 degrees. In the following **Schwanhof**, a downhill slope with an eleven percent grade puts stress on the brakes before you reach the 2154 again in Lösselmühle.

Turn left and you will reach Waidhaus after about five kilometres on a highly travelled street.

### Waidhaus

In 1989 the town name was known from the news: On December 23, the Foreign Ministers of the Czech Republic and the Federal Republic of Germany, Jiří Dienstbier and Hans-Dietrich Genscher, symbolically cut through the border fence near the border crossing. A memorial in Nové Domky (Bohemian Neuhäusl), two and a half kilometres north of the Czech Rozvadov, commemorates this historic act.

In Waidhausen turn left at the crossing of the B 14 (Hauptstraße) and

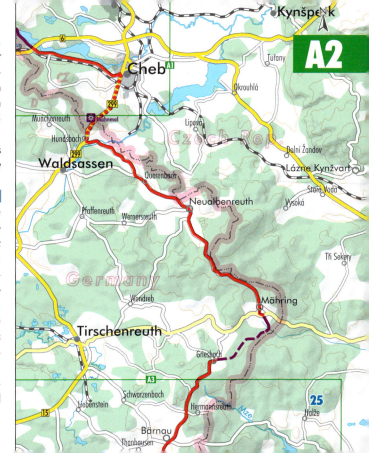

keep to the right where it continues to the left as the **Pilsener Straße**. The street **In der Au** becomes a brick road and leads, again as "Green Roof Cycle Trail", over the autobahn A 6. After the bridge the road makes a slight left and continues then straight ahead towards south through the forest. After one and half kilometres, you will reach the wetlands of the stream Pfreimd, which can be crossed on walkways and bridges. Hard to imagine that this is where the largest reservoir of the late Middle Ages once was! Continue further through the forest until you reach the 2154 again. Turn left and in two kilometres you will reach Eslarn.

### From Eslarn
### to Waldmünchen                                   45 km

From the church, continue to the left on the **Kirchstraße** and **Tillystraße**, until you reach the **Böhmer Straße** which takes you to the left. Continue on this road for about three kilometres until you reach the border crossing Tillyschanz.

## Tillyschanz

*Where today you find a colourful market square was once the town of Eisendorf (Železná). 90 percent of the buildings there were torn down. The historical Church of St. Barbara from the year 1770 also disappeared as well as the cemetery which made room for barracks. The snack bar and a small park by a pond invite to take a rest.*

Continue to the east over meadows and then on the D 197 through a forest slightly uphill and again downhill after the turn to **Smolov**. Make a right turn, continue through the long town and a further eight kilometres straight ahead until you reach Rybník (Waier).

## Rybník (Waier)

*The town has a small population. The Church of St. Anna was removed after the deterioration in 1964 and the townscape has been dominated by extensive agricultural facilities of the University of Pilsen since 1982. Here you can at least stock up on supplies or have a meal and spend the night.*

The route continues to the south to the village of **Závist** (Neid), which is in the middle of a clea-

ring. Continue to the right to **Novosedly** and Nemanice. After one kilometre, the paved road forks in the forest, which you will follow to the left. After a good ten kilometres, the road merges into a cross road where you keep to the right and continue into the valley through the meadows.

## Nemanice

*Since Nemanice (Wassersuppen) was in the restriction zone of the border and only accessible with special authorization, it increasingly deteriorated behind the double wire fence.*

Follow the road to the south through the town and you will directly come to the border crossing **Lísková** (Haselback) on the D 189, where you turn right.

*The village is completely gone and the once important border crossing which existed until 1990 is no longer present. Today it is highly visited and there are numerous shopping and dining possibilities on the Czech side of the border.*

On the German side, the 2146 makes a turn towards the south. On the cycle trail you will reach Waldmünchen without difficulties.

## Waldmünchen

The city with a population of 7,000 was granted city rights in 1250 and was under changing in the following years. Its fate was also very alternating: Escalade and plundering by the Hussites in 1434, several devastating city fires, plundering and pest epidemic during the Thirty Years War. They then struck lucky in 1742: The Baron Trenck occupied the city during the Austrian war of Succession, however did not plunder the city thanks to pleas from a priest and several school children. This occurrence has been the subject of the theatre performances of 300 actors since 1950 "Trenck der Pandur vor Waldmünchen" which are held in July and August every year with wild knight scenes and burning campfires (www.trenckfestspiele.de).

The climatic spa offers accommodation as well as dining and shopping possibilities. The Türmerstube in the city tower St. Stephan, which was occupied until 1923,

is worth visiting. Since 2001, a Borderland and Trenck Museum exist.

Trains depart from the local station directly to Cham and Prague.

### From Waldmünchen to Bayerisch Eisenstein                    70 km

From the marketplace, continue on the **Hammerstraße** to the south. Turn left in front of the modern clinic building into the **Krankenhausstraße** (2154) and then left again into the **Ulrichsgrüner Straße**. This leads you over an open area with good pavement through the town of the same name and then through sections of forest until you reach **Unterhütte** and **Althütte**. Althütte lies in a clearing and the visitors are made to climb. You can relax a bit on a level stretch before you reach a curvy section with a ten percent downhill grade which requires your attention. You can reward yourself in the restaurant Voithenberg on the left or four kilometres later in Furth im

Wald. Due to the proximity to the border and the frequent railroad traffic, the train station is rather large. The wide tracks separate the northern part of town from the historical centre. Once you have crossed them by the Glashütte (now FLBEG GmbH), keep to the left to the city square.

## Furth im Wald

*Furth was granted city rights in 1332. The history is not only presented in various museums but also in the Further Drachenstich. This is, the oldest performance in Germany and is presented from the second to the third Sunday every August. It consists of a parade with over 1,000 participants and 250 horses as well as a festival in which a dragon must die as symbol of defeating evil. As of 2010, the world's largest four-legged robot is planned to be used.*

*The baroque Church of Assumption of St. Maria influences the appearance of the city as well as the city tower which houses various museums including the first German Dragon Museum. The historic corridors below the city can be viewed from the Kramerstraße (May to September, daily 13:00 to 16:00).*

Trains depart from the local station directly to Schwandorf and Prague.

Leave the city on the **Eschlkamer Straße** to the east, and turn left shortly afterwards. Pass the recently dammed Drachensee and continue over the open area to **Geishof** via **Ösbühl** and **Daberg**. About two kilometres further you will reach **Schachten** and soon you will reach the 2140 which you will follow to the right for 500 metres and then turn left again. You will reach the 2154 heading southeast via **Seugenhof** and **Stachesried**.

*You can have a look at the land castle in the town from the 17th century. It once belonged to a son of Johann Gottfried Herder, who had studied agriculture but was very successful as estate manager. The promotion to nobility protected the heavily indebted estate from the attack of other nobles, but not from the law.*

*Four kilometres further you will reach Neukirchen beim Heiligen Blut.*

## Neukirchen beim Heiligen Blut

*A popular place of pilgrimage with a population of about 4,000. Apart from the Church of Pilgrimage at the beginning of town, you will also find the Klosterhof Hotel, a couple of restaurants and a supermarket.*

*You can also rest in **Mais** before you conquer the climb through the forest. You might prefer to pay a rewarding visit to the restaurant on top in **Absetz** before you continue downhill to **Buchetbühl**, **Engelshütt** and **Lam**. Here you will cross the Weißen Regen and keep to the left towards Lohberg. Continue along the river to **Lohberghütte** where you will find* accommodation and cafés and then on up to Lohberg.

## Lohberg

The town had a first glass hut in 1538, later many more. Following this tradition, the renowned glass sculptor Theodor Sellner opened a studio for artistic glass 460 years later. In the "Glashütte Alte Kirche" you can view the workshop and an exhibition (Brennesstraße 1). Not far away (Weideweg 5) the "Scharzauer Haus" presents pictures and glasses from two and a half centuries. In the adjacent farmer's store you can obtain regional products.

And now it becomes tiring. The **Arberstraße** leads up to **Altlohberghütte** and further up to 1,050 metres above sea level to the cross country ski centre of **Scheiben**.

At almost the same height you will also find the Hindenburgkanzel, a rock projection which was formed during the construction of the street and has an ob-

servation platform. The view reaches far over the Lamer Winkel from where you came. The summer can be rather short up here and you can expect late or early snow between the seasons.

The descend of 300 altitude metres begins by the sport hotel in **Brennes** and seven curvy kilometres to Bayerisch Eisenstein.

## Bayerisch Eisenstein

The name of the area originated from the former mining of iron ore. In the 18th century however, the glass industry was mainly responsible for the economic thriving. Due to the abundance of snow, the winter tourism has now become a decisive factor. It is worth paying a visit to the neo Baroque Church of St. Johannes Nepomuk with its wooden rococo sculptures. The largest attraction in Bayerisch Eisenstein however is the border train station which was built in 1877, half on German territory and half on Czech territory. The stretch was planned as

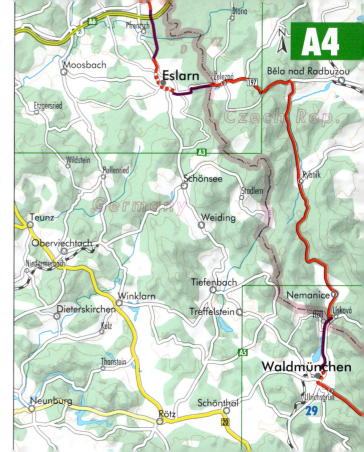

the shortest connection between Munich and Prague, was however not very effective due to the steep hills and sharp curves. Therefore no train traffic crossing the border has taken place since 1900.

The Iron Curtain also separated the train station: a wire fence separated the tracks as of 1953 and new wall were installed in the building. Since 1991 it is possible to change trains here and continue the journey in a different state.

Trains depart from the local station directly to Plattling and Prague.

## From Bayerisch Eisenstein to Aigen (Austria) | 140 km

Two and a half kilometres after Bayerisch Eisenstein, the counterpart, Železná Ruda (Markt Eisenstein) has a very similar history.

### Železná Ruda

It lies in the biosphere reserve Šumava (Böhmerwald) and profits from the vicinity to the 1,200 meter high Špiák (Spitzberg) and the ski areas. The city has many ela-

*Bayerisch Eisenstein - Train station and border*

borate villas, the landmark however is the baroque church Mariä Hilf vom Stern with its hexagram foundation and the massive central cupola. The rare late baroque altar cross is made of sanded and engraved ruby glass.

Continue on the E 53 towards Pilsen until the 190 makes a right towards Hartmanice after five kilometres. Follow the road for nine kilometres through a forest area past Nová Hrka and turn right again by Skelna. After about seven kilometres the paved road becomes a cobblestone road to the south towards Prášily (Stubenbach).

### Prášily (Stubenbach)

The scarcely populated area was declared a military restriction zone after 1948 and Prášily formed the centre of the troop exercise area. Tank roads and shooting ranges were created all around and the deserted villages were used as shooting targets. After the withdrawal of the military in 1991, the community Prášily was newly founded with the remaining 25 houses and has since then been striving to build an infrastructure to regain the once good reputation as a winter sport centre.

Here the road turns to the east again with alternating pavement until you reach Srní (Rehberg).

### Srní (Rehberg)

The area around this community founded by lumberjacks was so poor at the beginning of the 19th century that many people moved away. The Chinitz-Tettauer flume (Vchynicko-Tetovský plavební kanál) is maintained as a technical memorial from this time, which merges into the Kemelná. It runs from Modrava over about 15 kilometres, five thereof are underground, and served for rafting timber until 1958. It crosses under the road about two kilometres before Srní and to the right you can follow it for several kilometres on a signposted cycle trail.

Turn towards the south at the church. From **Antygl** the forested stretch continues along the Vydra from which the artistic, wooden 72 metre long Rechle Bridge separates from the flume. In **Modrava** (Mader), there is now an official population of 52. That is no comparison to the 2,000 German residents before the war.

Three kilometres northwest you will find the upland moor **Dreiseenfilz** (Tíjezerní sla) that can be accessed via plank walkways and is part of the large upland moor complex Maderer Filze. If you take a look to the west and south, you will recognize the pine forests that have been destroyed by pine beetles, which have be left to regenerate themselves.

Continue uphill to the east until you have reached Kvilda (Außergefilde) at an elevation of 1,065 metres.

## Kvilda (Außergefild)

Here you will find accommodation and numerous dining possibilities. The village became known

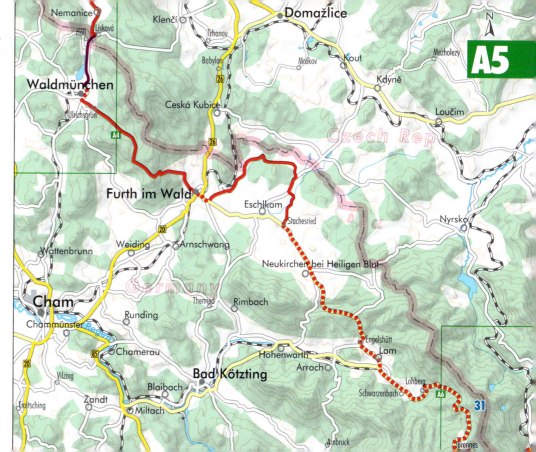

worldwide in the beginning of the 19th century by the tone wood company Strunz which still exists in Bavaria today. They were the first to provide pine wood for the production of instruments in the thick pine forests of the high elevations. A further unusual business was founded by Michael Verderber with the behind-glass painting of religious motives which his son continued to produce in large amounts. Apparently he produced 30,000 to 40,000 paintings annually. The museum of local history in the City Hall focuses on these two traditions.

The 167 continues slightly downhill to **Borová Ladaš** (Ferchenhaid) via **Františkov**. One kilometre to the north you will find the highland moor **Chalupská slať** (Großer Königsfilz), the largest moor lake of the Czech Republic with floating islands and rare vegetation which can be observed along the educational trail. Turn left in the village and the route continues in a very similar manner accompanied on the right side by the Warme Moldau (Teplá Vltava). Several kilometres ahead it merges with the Kalten Moldau by **Chlum** which also runs along the stretch later and together form the Moldau.

Marco Bertram "on the road"

In a sharp left curve, which forces the traveller from the south to the north direction for a short time, was once the location of the village **Polka** (Elendbachel), of which now only a mill pond exists to the right behind the stream.

Four kilometres further the road runs into the 4 in **Horní Vltavice** (Obermoldau). Follow the road to the right for about 500 metres and then turn left in a right curve by the baroque church into a smaller paved road to **Zátoň**.

**Tip:** If you would like to visit the bridge with the small Nepomuk chapel, which is under monument protection, you must take a 300 metre detour after the curve.

Continue below **Pažení** (1,281 m) which is to the left. The railroad stretch Vimperk-Volary passes here on the cliff in the forest.

*Parallel thereto you will find a fortification line of the Czechoslovakian wall which was built in the 1930's to prevent an expected attack by the Germans. It was modelled on the Maginot Line and was considered nearly impossible to overcome. However, in 1938, at the time on the Munich Agreement, it was only half completed and had to be given up upon.*

Turn right in **Zátoň** and after about five kilometres with a slight downhill grade through an open area, you will reach **Lenora** (Eleonorenhain).

The road makes a sharp turn into the 39 where you continue to the south.

*The small castle you will see ahead of you once belonged to the noble owner of the glass cabin, which the town thanks for its development as of 1834 and which also continues to produce today. The large, neo baroque house on the left at the end of town is called the Bienenhaus because a large number of glass making families lived here in small apartments like bees.*

400 metres further the road continues close to the shores of the Warmen Moldau. Here the Rechle leads over the river, a covered wooden bridge, which once served to control the floating wood in the river bend.

Continue five kilometres towards Volary with the forest on your left and the meandering river on the right. The road parts from the Moldau River in **Soumarský Most**. Turn right here over the river, past the campgrounds and further towards southwest through the forest until you reach České Žleby (Böhmisch-Röhren), which only consists of a few houses.

## České Žleby (Böhmisch-Röhren)

*Before the war, the village had a population of 1,200. After the expulsion of the Germans, it was hardly populated so that the church and the restaurants deteriorated until the centre of town was levelled in 1966.*

The route makes a left here. Continue along the edge of the forest almost the entire way to **Stožec** (Tusset) until you meet the Kalte Moldau (Studená Vltava) in the valley and turn right.

For those interested in romance and folk tradition, you will find the wooden **Tusset chapel** (Stožecká kaple) from 1791 to the north of the community on a mountainside. Several hotels offer the last accommodation before the German border.

It is only a further 4 kilometres for hikers and cyclists in the town of **Nové Údolí** (Neuthal).

The railroad line was extended to the border again on the Czech side in 1990. The continuation to Passau however cannot be restored due to the declassification of the stretch. This provided the possibility for "the shortest international railroad of the world" with a length of 105 metres: on the remaining streetch of the old railroad embankment, you can travel several metres into Germany with a small train from the Czech Republic; however you are not able to get off there. The travel time is 24 seconds! In three old freight train cars you will find a small railroad museum.

**Haidmühle** by the Kalten Moldau is a nationally recognised resort town with an elevation of 830 metres. There is a wide offer of accommodation. The 2130 continues from here uphill to the south towards Frauenberg.

**Iron Curtain Trail memorial**

It continues somewhat downhill after **Altreichenau** and reaches Neureichenau a few kilometres later.

## Neureichenau

Also a nationally recognised resort with a population of 4,400 at 670 meters above sea level at the foot of the Dreisessel (1,312 m).

Turn left about 500 metres after the church towards Riedelsbach. Continue slightly uphill through forests, past the manor Riedelsbach to the Rosenberger manor via **Riedelsbach** where you turn right towards Lackenhäuser before the campground. Here you will run into the 2630 which leads to the German-

Austrian border on the left in a few hundred metres. You can continue to Schwarzenberg am Böhmerwald without any controls.

## Schwarzenberg am Böhmerwald

A community of the upper Mühlviertels, which also thanks the glass production for its development.

Continue on the road which leads downhill through fields and meadows and reaches the town of Ulrichsberg via Klaffer am Hochficht.

## Ulrichsberg

It exists since 1325 at an elevation of 626 metres in the Tal der Großen Mühl and now has a population of about 3,000. For cyclists who have already experiences large parts of the Bohemian Forest will surely be interested in the 20 square metre large relief of Bohemian Forest which can be found in the tourist office at the market. For those who prefer to see it live, climb the 24 metre high observation tower Moldaublick on the Sulzberg which provides you with a view of the Moldau reservoir to the east. Apart from the church there is also a museum of local history which concerns the regional businesses. Unexpected to this area is a heartland of Jazz. The Jazz studio Ulrichsberg has arranged Jazz concerts every year for the past 30 years and the annual international music festival Ulrichsberger Kalaidophon (www.jazzatelier.at).

The street **Markt** turns into the **Falkensteinstraße** which you follow to the southeast to Schlägl via **Mühlberg** and **Zaglau**.

## Schlägl

## The history of Austria

Origin of the current population of Austria is the Bavarii and Germanic tribes which populated the territory of the current country after the fall of the Roman Empire. After the 8th century, the area mainly belonged to the Frankish kingdom of Charlemagne, whereby as of 1278 the Habsburg Empire developed a special position and advanced to a powerful factor in the Holy Roman Empire.

From the late 15th century to the end of the 17th century, the areas of the current Austria were continuously subject to attacks, especially from the Ottoman Empire which strived to the west from Hungary. The attempts of the Ottoman to expand however failed in 1683 in the second occupation of Vienna.

After numerous internal conflicts, Francis II was successful in founding the Austrian Empire in 1804. He accepted the title of Emperor as Franz I, whereby he was also the ruler of the Holy Roman Empire of the German Nation for two years. He had to resign from this title however in 1806 due to pressure from Napoleon and thus dissolve the Holy Roman Empire.

The new Austrian Empire was a multiethnic state, which was strictly ruled by Metternich. Target of the leadership was the restoration of the old order after the revolutionary disorder of the late 18th century, which mostly was a success in alliance with Prussia and Russia.

The inability to adapt to the drastic changes of the 19th century led to the revolution of 1848. The Metternich era was over. Finally the army prevented the victory of the democratic powers. The emperor however increasingly lost power and was forced to change the country into a constitutional monarchy and to grant Hungary new rights in the Compromise of 1867.

This formally created an Austrian-Hungarian double monarchy which had significant power in southeast Europe. After the assassination of the Austrian-Hungarian heir to the throne, Franz Ferdinand, the monarchy was very involved in the outbreak of World War I due to the mutual assistance pact. The defeat resulted in the dissolution of the Habsburg monarchy in 1918.

Successor was the new Republic of Austria, which was organised democratically and encouraged significant social progress. The young republic was however not of long duration: The Natio-

Border by
Schwarzenberg am Böhmerwald

nal Socialists who were then ruling the German Empire applied massive pressure and annexed Austria in 1938 as an integral part in their empire.

After the defeat of the Germans, Austria again became an independent, democratic country although it was divided into occupational zones until 1955, as Germany as well, of which most were Soviet.

Contrary to Germany, Austria was not subject to a division: After the signing of the Austria State Treaty on May 15, 1955 and the (not included in the contract) assurance of neutrality toward the western and eastern camp, the republic was granted its full sovereignty in 1955. The principle of the freedom from alliances anchored Austria in a "Conclusion of continuous neutrality" and complied with it until the end of the Cold War.

After the fall of the Iron Curtain, the country loosened its neutrality politics and oriented itself more

towards the west which was also evidenced by the joining of the EU in 1995. Until now, Austria is not a member of NATO – a result of its special role in the Cold War.

## Schlägl

The town is dominated by the Premonstratensian Monastery originating from the 13th century which applied over a long period, not only visually. Even today the monastery is considered a holy and economic centre of the upper Mühlviertels. It was provided with generous gifts and could be reconstructed after destruction by the Hussites, rebellious farmers and by three devastating fires. The privilege of the lucrative salt trade to Bohemia provided the facilities with the basis for expansion and cultural flourishing. The monastery offers visitors numerous dining facilities and tours, for example through the library comprising 60,000 books, the picture gallery with valuable paintings from the gothic to the romantic and the only monastery brewery in Austria.

The buildings of Schlägl continue to the north in the former monastery town on Aigen im Mühlkreis.

## Aigen

# From Aigen (A) to Bratislava

305 km

## From Aigen (Austria) to Vyssí Brod (Czech Republic)          50 km

### Aigen

Founded on monastery territory, the Eigen, the town grew quickly in its early years and has today developed into a tourist centre. This naturally means that there are good shopping possibilities.

Trains depart directly to Linz from the local train station. Both towns have a road connection to Baureith where you turn left towards Wurmbrand. The narrow paved road winds uphill and leads to Günterreith along the edge of the forest and further on to Sattling and St. Oswald bei Haslach.

### St. Oswald bei Haslach

**Tip:** It is worth taking a break in this town, but it is recommended to take a one kilometre detour over the fields to the east. Continue about 100 metres through the forest and you will find the Schwarzenberg flume which is also the border.

"Welcome to Austria!"

### Schwarzenberg flume

This engineering technical work was once, as well as other construction of the 18th and 19th century, considered the eighth wonder of the world since it was nothing less than the overcoming of the European water divide between Moldau and Danube, and thus between the Baltic Sea and the Black Sea. The flume began, supplied by several streams, in the northwestern Jelení Vrchy (Hirschbergen) on the north side of the Bohemian Forest which became the most important lumber supplier for Vienna. North of Haslach, the large pieces of wood were taken over by the Großen Mühl and transported to the Danube. The trade was

so successful that a northwesters increase to 52 kilometres was performed around 1820 whereby the flume was lead through a 419 metre long tunnel in Jelení Vrchy. Forest workers had to be hired and numerous new villages were formed in the border area. After 100 years in which hard workers brought approximately eight million cubic metres of wood along the way, the demand sank to the advantage of the Silesian coal. The system was therefore developed on the Czech side around 1900 for the transportation of logs and was in operation until 1961. Today large sections are restored as architectural monuments and are used by tourists for demonstrations and for raft festivals. The escarpment in Morau, to the east of St. Oswald, belongs to the most impressive since the water is especially powerful and loud here. The historical road accompanying the flume is signposted as a cycle trail and leads through some of the most beautiful areas of the Bohemian Forest.

The Iron Curtain Trail continues to the south gently downhill via **Almesberg** until shortly before you reach Damreith where it meets the

connecting road between Aigen and Haslach in a sharp corner. Make a sharp left turn uphill to **Oedt** via **Unterurasch** and again downhill towards **Hinternberg**. Where the cycle trail R5 turns left to the sawmill Zach, turn left towards Innenschlag. The narrow paved road makes a right and leads to **St. Stefan am Walde** via **Dambergschlag**. With some downhill areas, you will leave the plateau via **Herrnschlag**, **Afiesl** and **Köckendorf** to Guglwald.

## Guglwald

*This town appears to exist entirely of one hotel complex in which the pagoda style, Middle Age aspiration and folklore have been joint together. The journey continues over the adjacent border into the Czech Republic. Before you cross the border, however, you should continue 400 metres further to the right along the border where you will find a memorial of the Iron Curtain under a concrete roof with various information plaques and original artefacts of the former border fence.*

Continue five kilometres to the north on a smooth stretch. Afterwards you must have a lot

**Iron Curtain Trail Memorial**

of trust in your brakes since a 12 % grade leads you downhill to Přední Vítoň (Vorder Heuraffl) by the Lipno reservoir.

## Přední Vítoň (Vorder Heuraffl)

*The village, which had to sacrifice the lower ground to the reservoir in the 1950's, was founded in the 14th century by two hermitages from which a monastery was formed. The later reconstructed and renovated church is from this period. Unfortunately the interior was stolen. A hotel and numerous guest houses offer overnight accommodation.*

Turn right and you will have a beautiful view of the lake and good road conditions for the

next ten kilometres until you reach the dam. Afterwards continue on the right shore of the Moldau until you reach Loučovice (Kienberg).

## Loučovice (Kienberg)

*A paper factory which has existed here for 125 years, which mainly belongs to the Czech Republic, greatly influences the appearance of this community.*

The street cuts a curve of the Moldau heading north and thereby follows the original path of the river.

*Prior to the completion of the reservoir, there was white water here formed by massive rocks, the* **Teufelsströme**, *which was narrowed by the Čertova stěna (Teufelswand). Large sections of the steep cliffs of this chasm are covered with gravel and the elevations crowned with massive boulder formations. The area is a national reserve with its unique and valuable flora and fauna. It is however accessible to pedestrians from a parking area.*

## Vyšší Brod (Hohenfurth)

*Below the small equalising reservoir which is characterised as Lipno II, you will find the small* town of Vyšší Brod (Hohenfurth). It is especially known for it's cloister which you will pass upon entering. The community on a passage over the Moldau served for observation of a trade route from the middle of the 13th century. Its fate was closely related to that of the wealthy cloister which it belonged to until 1848. Its economic activities at the beginning of the 20th century included the construction of an electrical power plant and the participation in the construction and operation of the electrical railway. It was discontinued after the annexation of Sudetenland, and then again founded after the war. Weakened by the expulsion of the German members of the convent, it was not able to resist the attacks from the national side so that it was again discontinued in 1950. The building served as a military barracks and was later partially subject to deterioration. After a poor beginning, visitors are now able to view the gothic church, the cloister, the chapter house, the baroque library and the art objects of the monastery collection.

Trains depart directly to Rybnik from the local train station.

## From Vyšší Brod (Czech Republic) to Gmünd (Austria)                    80 km

Follow the 163, and thus also the Moldau, for about one kilometre via the market place towards the west and then turn right after a petrol station towards Horní Dvoriste. Here you will find the cycle route, Šumavská magistrála, which leads uphill as a narrow paved road. Keep to the left at the fork in the road on the gravel road and you will reach **Dolní Drkolá** via a forest and mountain meadow. Turn left at this village which appears to be completely lost and you will reach Horní Dvořiště (Oberhaid).

## Horní Dvořiště (Oberhaid)

Turn left before you reach the triangular village square and you will again reach the 163 after three kilometres on a well paved road.

Although the traffic becomes heavier, you will make good progress to Dolní Dvořiště (Unterhaid) on the smooth Birkenallee.

## Dolní Dvořiště (Unterhaid)

Here it is worth paying a visit to the late gothic St. Gilles Church and the fountain at the market place and the statue of St. Nepomuk.

For the further journey, orient yourself to the north and then to the west according to the signposted cycle trail 34.

After about two and a half kilometres on a quiet route, you will cross the Maltsch and see the gothic church of St. Ondrej of **Rychnov nad Malší** (Reichenau) where you turn right. Holy figures on the side of the road announce the Pilgrimage Church of Our Lady of the Snows (Svatý Kámen).

## Our Lady of the Snows (Svatý Kámen)

It was built over a stone in the shape of a chair and reopened in 1993 after a period of deterioration. The Tichá is quickly reached from here which is characterised by a row of abandoned houses but also by an angular tower, the remains of a fortification from the Middle Ages by a small lake.

The further route towards the south is partially in poor condition which is however compensated for by the interesting destination. This is the settlement location of the abandoned town of Cetviny (Zettwing) directly on the border to Austria which is marked here by the Maltsch.

## Settlement location of the abandoned village Cetviny (Zettwing)

*All but four of the 120 houses of the village which deteriorated after the expulsion were levelled in 1955/56. That what remained was used by the border police, including the church tower which served as an observation tower. Personalities and organisations from the Czech Republic and Austria arranged the restoration of the early gothic church ruins as of 1995, which was performed very carefully and revealed unknown frescos. In 2003, the building was re-inaugurated. The building is accessible from both sides of the border for various purposes.*

At a crossing four kilometres further, leave the road to the right and continue towards Nové Hrady (39 kilometres) and continue to follow the cycle trail 34. Continue through the lonesome forests and over mountain meadows and on very differing grounds through the deserted village of **Dolní Přibrání** where you will also find a war memorial commemorating the small village of **Leo-poldov**. There the route 34 makes a right, however keep to the left towards **Pohorská Ves**, continue through the town and keep to the right at the fork in the road. After a quick ride on a level road through the forest, turn right over the Černá (Schwarzau) and through **Černé Údolí** where you will find a small gust house. Turn left at the fork in the road after the settlement. A longer stretch of forest follows until the landscape opens up shortly before you reach Horní Stropnice (Strobnitz).

## Horní Stropnice (Strobnitz)

*The community that you will enter on the long old village green has been populated since the end of the 12th century. There were two economic mills, an engine works and an important brewery, as well as the tourism since about 1850. The slender statue of the Virgin Mary on the market place cannot be overseen and also the originally Roman Church of St. Nicholas greets you from the distance. The interior was recently extensively restored and shines with a Renaissance altar, baroque side altars and a rococo pulpit.*

It is not easy to leave Horní Stropnice since the 154 has an uphill grade of twelve percent here. After less than three kilometres you will reach Světví.

## Světví

**Tip:** If you are looking for a place to take a break, you can make a 500 metre detour to the left to the Cukštejn fortress (Zuckenstein).

## Cukštejn (Zuckenstein)

*The late gothic residence is surrounded by a moat on an elevation above the Strobnitz. It is gradually being renovated by the new private owner and provides tired cyclists with refreshments.*

*The Terčino údolí (Theresiental) accompanies the river.*

## Terčino údolí (Theresiental)

*In 1756, the 140 hectare area was turned into a park. Various spas from the 19th century and an even older hammer mill are maintained as well as a romantic artificial waterfall.*

Those who have decided to take this little detour can return to the old route two kilometres further to the north so there are hardly any additional kilometres to travel.

## Nové Hrady (Gratzen)

A little further you will ride around the ring shaped fortress of Nové Hrady (Gratzen). The largest moat of Bohemia was not able to protect it from numerous pillages. It is once again accessible after the renovation work and offers a good overview of the medieval construction of the little town at its feet. The low fourth last house on the right before the gate is the 300 year old blacksmith's shop of the family Gossinger (Novohradská kovárna) which was renovated several years again and used for demonstrations of the old trade. From the castle, you will reach the market place straight ahead which has a late baroque fountain. The opposite east side is occupied by the early baroque residence of the Count of Bucquoy. It was constructed by the connection of originally independent manors to a complex and is now operated as a wellness hotel. The Renaissance city hall on the west side also houses the tourist information office. In a nearby renovated house, the baroque apothecary was reopened after more than 30 thirty years. Past the residence on the right you will reach the baroque

church of St. Peter and Paul and the monastery of the same name which served as shelter for the border guards during the Cold War. The garden of the New Castle separates the old and new town, for which the residence in the town was given up in 1810.

Continue straight ahead and make a slight left at the crossing on the **Zahradní čtvrť** (Gartenviertel) in order to leave the town towards Ceské Velenice and Gmünd. Continue through fields via **Nakolice** until you reach **Vyšné**, then ten kilometres of forest follow. At the end, you will cross over two railroad tracks and meet the 103. It leads to the right, parallel to the railroad to Česke Velenice (Gmünd railway station, formerly Unterwielands).

## Česke Velenice

What is now an independent city with a population of 3,400, originated on the farmlands of the village Wieland to the southwest as an engine shed of the Kaiser-Franz-Josef Railway (between Vienna and Prague) and as a railway station for the Austrian city of Gmünd, which is directly opposite on the other side of the Lainsitz. A new district developed rapidly from

At the border to Gmünd

a small settlement. After the dissolution of the Austro-Hungarian Empire, the newly formed Czechoslovakia received the border areas in 1920 whereby the Lainsitz became the border river and the railroad station of Gmünd became a Czech city. The largest employer is still the railroad, but with an industrial park that reaches over the border they are hoping for additional impulses.

After a few hundred metres parallel to the river you will reach the border crossing and thus Gmünd. From the crossing you will almost automatically reach the long town square. Before you follow the left curve in the road, you have a view of the oldest building on the right, the city castle, which goes back to the 12th century although it has been altered numerous times.

## Gmünd

The preserved zone of the town square is dominated by the old City Hall from the early Renaissance which is in the middle. The museum on the 1st floor offers a multimedia presentation of the history of the city. The café on the tower side of the City Hall is very popular. If you however have a seat at the Boulevard Café on the opposite side, you will be sitting right in front of the architectonic highlights of the town, the two Sgraffito houses from the 16th century. The left facade, unique in Austria, is covered with rich ornaments, the other with antique heroic saga themes and both are crowned with pinnacles.

If you are an enthusiast of unusual geological formations, you should take a trip into the Blockheide along the Braunaubach (Brown Meadow-Stream) which flows to the east of the old town. It indeed lives up to it's name: It is characterised by massive, often loose, piled-up granite blocks, which had formed underground and were then lifted to the surface. The climb to the observation tower leads through underground rooms with the adventure exhibition "The birth of the wobbly stones".

Trains depart directly to Ceské Budejovice from the local train station.

The **Litschauer Straße**, which leads into the city, also leads out of the city and determines one of the next intermediate targets. This time you will not cross over the border again but rather turn right before the border just after crossing the Lainsitz. After the Czech-German industrial park, again cross the meandering Lainsitz and soon afterwards you will be in the vicinity of the Czech border again in a large right curve. Before you reach **Neu-Nagelberg**, cross the narrow gauge railroad and the E 49 next to the border, continue through the town and you will reach a peaceful forest area to **Alt-Nagelberg** after the numerous ponds of the dammed Gamsbach.

*The following town Brand (blaze) got its name from a large forest fire in 1666.*

At the fork in the road, keep to the left towards Gopprechts and Litschau (10 km). After

Litschau

**Gopprechts**, which is to the right of the road, you will be accompanied by the stream Reißbach and the narrow gauge railroad through meadows, forests and wetlands, which is a very interesting mixture. After the Schönauer pond and the castle, which is under private ownership, you will reach Litschau, the most northern city of Austria.

## Litschau

*The road makes a right turn and, similar to Gmünd, you will reach a long town square, the centre of which is occupied by the Church of St. Michael. Litschau is the final stop of a narrow*

gauge railroad that is used during the summer as a museum. You can find numerous shopping and dining possibilities here. The Reißbach is dammed here and forms the long, curvy and attractive manor pond to the north.

The town square continues to the east in the **Reitzenschläger Straße** which leads to the town of the same name. You will come to a fork in the road and continue to the left past several of the numerous ponds which are joined together to long bands in some locations. Turn left on the Waidenhofener Bundesstraße (5) and shortly afterwards again to the right. Leopoldsdorf is now in front of you. Continue 400 metres after the pond and then turn left towards Kautzen. At the merging of the road, next to a further pond, turn left towards **Kautzen** via **Reinberg**, **Dobersberg** and **Radschin**.

*Before you reach the village, you will pass **Illmau** with its Renaissance castle. The previous construction once served as a border protection and the community of Kautzen, which has been populated since the 12th century, was the main seat of the ruling party. The three-winged castle is partially in ruins and cannot be visited since it is under private ownership.*

## Kautzen

*Kautzen received several awards for its efforts in renewing the village and establishing sustainable energy sources (European village rejuvenation award, European solar prize, Lower Austrian environmental award).*

The **Thayatal Bundesstraße** (30) towards Dobersberg brings the cyclists into the valley of the Taxenbach and in venturous curves to **Tiefenbach**. You have a wide view over the fields to Dobersberg, which you will reach in a further eight kilometres.

## Dobersberg

*The community flourished due to its function as a river crossing point over the German Thaya and its location as a cross-point between two trade roads. At this crossing, the most characteristic points of interest are concentrated: the St. Lamberti Church with gothic core which was renovated in the 19th century, the pillory from the 17th century as symbol of the higher jurisdiction and the impressively large Renaissance castle with the dominant corner tower.*

At this crossing, turn towards the north. Continue on the **Waldkirchener Straße** for several hundred metres out of town and then to the right towards **Lexnitz**. The route continues on a paved cycle trail along the river, which first crosses the railroad tracks and then turns back through a tunnel. In a large angle over the fields you will reach **Waldkirchen an der Thaya**. Turn right here, continue through the town and further to Weikertschlag an der Thaya via **Waldhers** and **Wetzles**.

## Weikertschlag an der Thaya

*This time we refer to the Moravian Thaya, where the community already existed at the foot of a castle in the 12th century. Once a proud border fortification, it is now completely gone. The pillory at the market place, from which the "Prangerhansl" looks down, reminds of past times, although not as far back as the 12th century.*

Continue over the village greens out into the fields. 300 metres after the development, turn right at the fork in the road which means a slight uphill climb to **Schaditz**. The next town of **Luden** is rather lonely with direct contact to the border. In **Oberthürnau** you will come to a street which leads to the border crossing on the left.

**Tip:** Those thinking about spending the night should turn right towards Drosendorf since accommodation is very limited in the small towns until Znojmo. The city is also worth paying a visit to.

## Drosendorf

*There is a guest house right at the beginning of town, but for those who prefer something special, you can also spend the night in the castle. This impressive construction with four wings was constructed in the 12th century to control the entrance to the city and rebuilt in early baroque style after a fire. It now houses a school and serves as a bed and breakfast throughout the year.*

*The town lies on a high cliff, which is surrounded by the Thaya on three sides. It dates back to the year 1200 and originally served as a border fortification against Moravia. It still shows how well-fortified it is today: it is the only Austrian city*

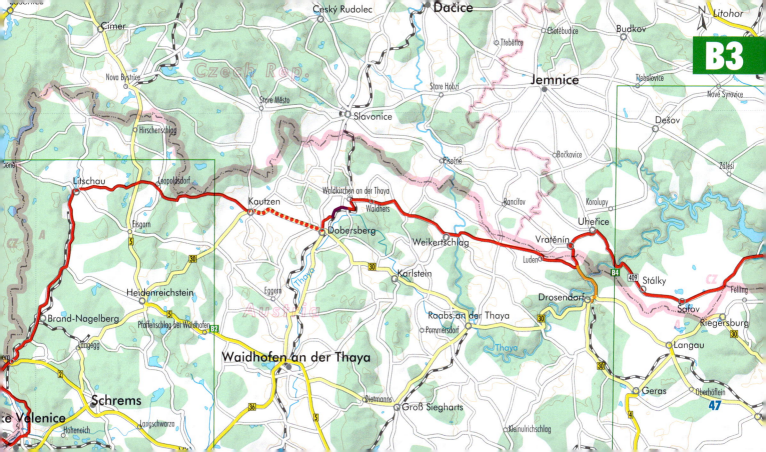

that is completely surrounded by a maintained city wall. The 1.7 kilometres with 14 towers, two gates and the respective moats are impressive to view during a walk on the promenade. The entire construction forms a long triangle due to the natural conditions which also applies to the main square. The foundation is occupied by the sgrafitto decorated City Hall where you will also find the information centre. The church is located in the centre, but the pillory of over eight metres is also noteworthy which is one of the highest of mid Europe and is not to be confused with the pillory column (Pestsäule) across from the City Hall. The building which towers over the others on the Schlossplatz is called the Stockkastl because it served as a prison in the 18th century. Cells with barred windows and iron doors from this period are still maintained on the first level. The building was originally the oldest Roman church and then served as a granary (Schüttkasten). The history of the city is not very "glorious": since the late Middle Ages, they had to surrender to their fiends at least eight times - which puts the value of fortification facilities in question, not only for pacifists.

Take the familiar route back to Oberthürnau and continue straight ahead over the border to Vratěnín (Fratting).

## Vratěnín (Fratting)

This community with a population of less than 300 once saw better times. Granted city rights in the Middle Ages, the town was the residence of a noble ruling surrounded by lodges and later the main postal station on the postal route from Vienna to Prague. The new Kaiserstraße lead further to the north so that many elaborate constructions deteriorated or became monuments: the former refuge (now a guesthouse), the post office (now the city hall) or the castle. Eager efforts lead to extensive beautification measures and 1996 to the title "Village of the Year".

For quite some time, newly planted rows of fruit trees reach in all directions, also to the east along the 409. It leads past small concrete bunkers on the field to Uhercice (Ungarschitz), around an elaborate Renaissance castle with numerous wings and a pond and then turns towards the south.

## Uherčice (Ungarschitz)

The building which served as barracks and a women's prison after 1945 is now partially in critical condition, was however declared a cultural monument in 2002.

After a level section the route becomes hilly and wooded. You will cross the Dyje (Thaya) and keep to the right, still on the 409, until you reach **Stálky** (Stallek) with its ethnic-fortifying appearing church tower - and unfortunately also the bumpy pavement. The principle of a rectangular meadow that runs through the entire town is also found four kilometres further in Šafov (Schaffa).

## Šafov (Schaffa)

Here the houses are much closer together. This is not surprising, as this village with a population of 170 was once considered a city-like settlement and has as such a very special history which reflects the large events of time on a smaller scale. The prospering village greatly suffered during the Thirty Years War. Vienna and Lower Austria were invaded in order to expel the Jewish population. The owner of Vranov (Frain) saw thereby an opportunity: He relocated 85 Jewish families to Šafov which belonged to his jurisdiction. Soon the Jews of Schaffa controlled the surrounding trade with linen, leather, wool and other raw materials. After the emancipation of the Jews in 1848, which was accompanied by freedom, and the construction of the railroad which allowed direct delivery of factories and markets, many of the Jews emigrated. In 1938, only 68 Jewish residents remained of the once 650, of which approximately half were not able to save themselves from the Nazi terror. The Czechs were forced to leave the town after the arrival of the Germans. The Germans were then forced to leave at the end of the war. Šafov had a population of exactly 1,251 in 1843 and in 1994 only 169.

The large construction with the green hipped roof, which you will see on the right upon entering the village, is the former synagogue from 1785. The well maintained Jewish cemetery lies diagonally across from it, thus to the left at the end of the village.

Memorial of the opening of the border

The route continues at the beginning of town. Continue on the 398 over the fields, past a Nepomuk column behind the settlement, past the old cemetery by Podmye to Vranov nad Dyjí (Frain an der Thaya).

## Vranov nad Dyjí (Frain an der Thaya)

**Tip:** Before a sharp left curve, you will find the castle complex on a high cliff. You should take the time to pay a visit. The street here leads down to the town in a wide curve without a direct connection between the town and the castle.

This large complex not only offers an impressive overall picture but also an interesting architectural history. The border fortress from the 11th century was renovated to a baroque castle as of 1680 by the famous architect Fischer von Erlach from Vienna. Thereby the Ancestors' Hall with its oval foundation was created, which appears especially prominent from the market square. Later the castle chapel was added on the left of the entrance. As of 1722, the large three-winged complex with the court of honour was added, which later received its classical appearance. In the 19th century, the oldest section of the castle received the mostly unavoidable neo-gothic amendments of this period. In the former carriage stall to the right of the entrance, you can view products of the stoneware production, which enjoyed recognition throughout Europe especially due to the Frainer Wegdwoodkeramik.

Continue downhill to the Thaya and over the bridge where you will be greeted by St. Nepomuk. The centre of the village lies in a sharp curve of the river which is dammed to a reservoir a little further up. After a left curve you will reach the market square and thereby circle around the elaborate Church of the Assumption of the Virgin Mary. Several buildings date back to the Middle Ages, which were later renovated in the baroque style. A valuable baroque memorial is the plague column, which reminds of the epidemic of 1680.

Continue your journey over the square and then a stretch of hard work follows. 900 metres long the street winds uphill until it reaches the top and leads to **Lesná** (Liliendorf) along the edge of the forest. At the end of the village, built along the road without gaps, you will find a restaurant in a large old windmill with good food and spectacular views.

Here you will come to a fork in the road where you keep to the right towards **Horní Břečkov** (Oberfröschau). Continue straight ahead through the town towards **Lukov**.

**Tip:** If you are willing to make a detour of three kilometres, turn right towards Cizov where a portion of the convoy road with the barbed wire fence and an observation tower

Znojmo

(špak) are well maintained.

Complete the triangle on the convoy road towards **Lukov** and follow the rows of fruit trees to Hradište (Pöltenberg) via **Podmolí** and **Mašovice** which already belong to Znojmo (Znaim).

**Tip:** Here you can again enjoy a view over the city from above before you continue down into the city.

## Hradiště

*Hradiště was an important fortification in the Great Moravian Empire of the 9th and 10th century and the complex of the late baroque*

church of St. Hippolyt with the monastery is located at the site of very old previous buildings.

A long curve brings you into the northwest suburb and to the **Svoboda Square**. Where the E 59 makes a left, continue straight ahead into the maze of the medieval alleyways in the Old Town.

## Znojmo (Znaim)

*The town lies on a plateau over the Thaya and you will find a fortification at the most advantageous strategic location. It was built at the end of the 12th century as a replacement for the castle Hradiště on the opposite side, which had become old-fashioned. The inner fort, which was surrounded by a moat in the 13th century, was later renovated to a baroque castle. The oldest parts of the original fortification include the rotunda of St. Catherine which is considered the most valuable cultural asset of the city. It contains unique wall paintings and, a picture cycle of biblical motifs, mixed with a gallery of Premyslid rulers. Similarly prominent on the high*

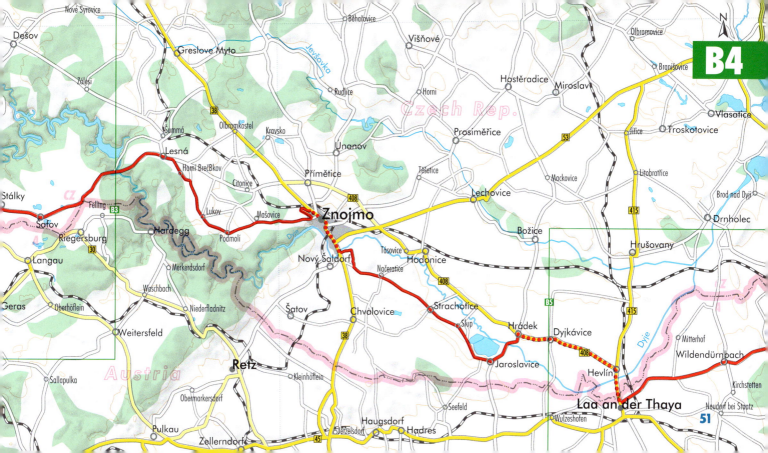

shore is the late gothic hall church of St. Nicholas, the interior of which was renovated during the baroque period but still contains gothic frescos. The northern tip of the old town pyramid was dominated by the Church of St. Michael, which was renovated in baroque. The tower was newly erected after the collapse on the chancel side, separated by a street. Between Horní námsti (Oberer Platz) and the long Masaryk Square, you will find the true landmark of the city – the 80 metre high late gothic tower of City Hall. The upper finishing forms a walkway with four corner towers and this construction is repeated further up, however turned 45 degrees and crowned by a slim tip - one of the most fascinating creations of the Czech late baroque. Numerous residential houses from the Renaissance and an extensive maze of underground tunnels belong to the points of interest of Znojmo which you should spend more than a day visiting (www.znojmocity.cz/de).

Trains depart from the local station directly to Vienna and Breclav.

## From Znojmo (Czech Republic) to Laa an der Thaya (Austria)          40 km

In order to leave the city to the south, you must follow the highly travelled E 59. It leads straight to the no longer controlled border crossing Hat-Kleinhaugsdorf.

### Hatě–Kleinhaugsdorf

It became internationally known by the historically meaningful and symbolic cutting of the border fence by the Foreign Ministers of Austria and the Czech Republic, Alois Mock and Jiří Dienstbier on December 17, 1989. The newly opened economic possibilities are ironically also expressed in the shopping and adventure site "Excalibur City".

The route of the Iron Curtain Trail branches to the left right after the Thaya bridge towards Bohumilice. After a small chapel at the second crossing, continue to the right over the fields. The narrow country road merges into an alley of fruit trees where you continue your journey to the left. It passes a small wine area through **Načeratice** and **Strachotice** towards Slup (Zulp).

### Slup (Zulp)

Here the narrow village green stretches to the left which runs with grand rows of trees toward a large building with a stately appearance. It is one of the water mills originating from the Renaissance and is the largest is Moravia with four functioning mill wheels. The old facility is just as interesting as the South Moravian mill museum on the upper level.

To the left you will find fish ponds which stretch over two kilometres and Jaroslavice (Joslowitz) lies at the end thereof.

### Jaroslavice (Joslowitz)

A large Renaissance castle in need of renovation thrones over the town. The complex with four wings is decorated with an elegant arcade with massive arches.

Cross over the Thaya once again and you will see a baroque church with colourful frescos upon entering **Hrádek** (Erdberg) which is surrounded by the protective walls of the no longer existing castle. At the same location you will also find an old rotunda from the Roman period. In Hrádek you will come to the 408.

To the right you will reach **Hevlín** (Höflein an der Thaya) via **Dyjákovice** (Groß Tajax). The 415 which runs to the south leads you straight to Laa an der Thaya.

## Laa an der Thaya

The Hauptstraße merges into the town square, the size of which is due to former military reasons: it was to serve for the gathering of army units during periods of war and fugitive residents of the surroundings. It has been dominated for a good hundred years by the eclectic new City Hall. Next to this, the old City Hall by the pillory column of 1575 – apart from its overwhelming splendour – appears almost cosy. The Kirchengasse branches off from the town square and leads to the church of St. Vitus in the east, a late Romanic basilica with baroque decorations. The northeast corner of the Kirchenplatz meets the Burgplatz, which once comprised the entire complex of houses on the left up to the Breiten Gasse and, like the town square, was also designed for the gathering of troops. From here you can reach the castle which was originally surrounded by

Laa an der Thaya - City Hall

water and designed as a place of final refuge. The round butter churn tower and residential buildings were added later.

The city which was founded around 1230 with martial intentions became continuously less important due to martial influences. This became even worse when it lost a large part of land due to the founding of Czechoslovakia in 1918. There have been numerous changes since the opening of the border: the number of visitors is increasing, especially after the opening of a so-called thermic resort. An electric train now also travels to Vienna, although not into the Czech Republic yet, and additionally the population has increased. There are also numerous shopping and, dining opportunities and you can find some excellent overnight accommodation. The restaurant Zur Goldenen Rose at the Stadtplatz 8 is reasonably priced.

### From Laa an der Thaya to Hohenau an der March                60 km

Leave the town to the north: 500 metres before you reach the border, the road branches off to the right towards Wildendürnbach. After 1.5 kilometres, you will suddenly find yourself between the fronts. On the right, displaced residents of Hevlín/Höflein commemorate the fallen of both World Wars and on the left the Russians have placed a memorial for their fallen soldiers. Continue a further 9 kilometres on the southern edge of **Wildendürnbach** and then on the northern edge of **Neuruppersdorf** and **Pottenhofen**. Turn left after passing the buildings. A little further you will reach the through street behind the church in the middle of the long town of **Ottenthal** where you then turn right. You will soon reach **Guttenbrunn** and continue over the fields again where the road makes a right curve after a small hill and then makes a fork. Follow the road to the right which is hilly, surrounded by vineyards and leads to Falkenstein.

## Falkenstein

*The village lies at the foot of an impressive limestone cliff on which a castle ruin thrones. The Kellergasse that leads out of the town to the southeast is special, to the right and left of which are not less than 65 pressing houses with adjacent underground cellars. If you are considering taking a rest here, you should be wary as it is not a coincidence that the street is called "Eiergasse" by the locals.*

*If you would like to visit the castle ruin, you must travel around the mountain to the northern side. Thereby you will pass a church. The early baroque nave of the church forms an attractive combination with the late Romanic tower. The Castle of Falkenstein was built around 1050 as a fortification. It has been under private ownership since 1572 and was first renovated*

*Ruins Falkenstein*

and later used as a quarry by the owner. In the summer the tournament grounds are used for festivals and performances.

At the roundabout at the beginning of town, take a sharp turn towards the east. The road is level so that it is accompanied by the Mühlbach which flows through the following town of **Poysbrunn**. Cross under the E 461 and you will reach Herrnbaumgarten, a community which has been known in the past to do some silly things.

## Herrnbaumgarten

*For those of you with a sense for "crazy" things, the nonsense museum and similar facilities are right for you.*

The route continues further towards **Schrattenberg**, where you will find the guesthouse Zesch for dining and/or overnight accommodation. Continue to the south on the **Schafzeile** over the fields and then along wetlands to **Katzelsdorf** and the 47. Turn right here for one kilometre, then leave the road again to the left. The very quiet road leads you to Altlichtenwarth, to the north of which you will find the Hutsaulberg.

## Altlichtenwarth

*The Hutsaulberg still has remains of a medieval fortification and a memorial commemorating the soldiers on a hill with an observation platform. It offers a wide view of the vineyards, to Moravia and to Slovakia.*

Turn left in the town and you will reach the village of Hohenau an der March via **Hausbrunn**, shortly before the triangle border of the Czech Republic, Austria and Slovakia.

## Hohenau an der March

*Since the opening of the border, an economic improvement has not yet been seen in the scarcely populated area which is in a less*

advantageous area. The closing of the 140 year old sugar factory in 2006 brought about the opposite effect. Also the newly opened bridge over the March, the only one north of the Danube, is also not very promising. In 2005 a single direction drawbridge was sufficient.

The appearance of the town is not very exciting. The bell tower of 1745 is considered the landmark which was moved to the northern edge of the city due to traffic reasons. The originally Roman church was renovated around 1700 in baroque and newly decorated. Of particular artistic value is the late baroque Barbara altar. The bird paradise formed in a vast and relatively warm cooling water pond of the sugar factory which also includes a research station is also in danger of closing.

### From Hohenau an der March (Austria) to Bratislava (Slovakia)          75 km

Continue over the March and into Slovakia from the southeast edge of town. The **Marchstraße** runs from the cooling water pond to the south to the new bridge.

Marchauen

**Tip**: The crossing can be flooded and closed if there is a slight elevation of water.

**Tip**: For those who do not want to continue the 28 kilometres on the Austrian side before transferring to the other side by ferry in Angern an der March, can take the 50 kilometre detour to the north via Beclav (Lundenburg) and make the best of it. The town with its history full of change is worth visiting. (The ferry in Angern also does not travel when the water level is high. The construction of a bridge is planned as of 2010. You should therefore inform yourself regarding the water levels and/or construction progress in advance.)

## The history of Slovakia

The Celts in the area of the current Slovakia were replaced in the first century after Christ by the Germanic Quads. Slovakia became a Germanic area on the border of the Roman Empire (1st-5th century) where numerous Roman-Quadic wars took place. Around 500, the Slavic ancestors of the current Slovacs appeared. In the 7th century, Slovakia was part of the main area of the Samo Empire. In the 8th century, the Principality of Nitra was formed here which became part of the main area of Great Moravia in 833.

In the 11th century, the area of the current area of Slovakia became part of the Hungarian Kingdom, which was part of the Habsburg Empire since 1526, the Austrian Empire since 1804 and Austria-Hungary since 1867.

After World War I, the first Czechoslovakian Republic was formed in 1918 which existed de facto until 1938. In the Munich Agreement, the areas with a majority of German population (Sudetenland) were assigned to the German

Empire in 1938. The southern portion of Slovakia and the Carpathian Ruthenia were assigned to Hungary, the Teschen area was occupied by Poland.

Slovakia became independent under the fascist Jozef Tiso for the first time from 1939 to 1945, was however in fact a satellite state of Hitler-Germany. After World War II, it once again became part of Czechoslovakia.

When Michael Gorbatschow became active for Glasnost and Perestroika in 1989, the communist government was forced to resign by the "Velvet Revolution". Václav Havel was elected first president of the Czech and Slovak Federal Republic (SFR) which existed from April 1990 to the end of 1992.

The Prime Minister of the Slovakian constituent republic, Vladimír Meiar, was the first Prime Minister of the constituent state to be elected in June 1990. On April 23, 1991, he was removed by parliament and replace by Ján Arnogurský. As a result, he formed the "Movement for a Democratic Slovakia" (HZDS) which won the Parliament election in June 1992. The negotiations of January 1, 1993 with Václav Klaus, who had won the election in the Czech territory, led to the division of the Czechoslovakia into two independent states – the Czech and Slovak Republics.

Slovakia became a member of NATO and the European Union in 2004.

On the road to Moravský Svätý Ján you will first reach the river embankment and somewhat later a cycle trail which follows a channel on which you continue the journey to the right. It is an evenly paved road which leads through corn, wheat and cabbage fields and is occasionally lined with trees. The landscape is stimulating and peaceful and you will see numerous herons and storks over the next 11.5 kilometres until you reach the road to Malé Leváre. Thereby, the Auwald along the March is always in view. Occasional barracks belong to the Czechoslovakian wall already mentioned in the Czech Horní Vltavice, the further construction of which had to be discontinued in 1939.

A reaction ferry travelled between Drösing and Veké Leváre for 300 years with a bar on each of the shores.

Cross the gravel road, which was once a connection road, 1.5 kilometres after the turn which leads to Zavod on the left. A little later you will pass an old border troop base which currently houses the largest military dog school in Slovakia. The pavement now becomes brittle and soon ends completely. You must travel over two kilometres on gravel and sand and the inhospitableness of the area is emphasised by remaining concrete bollards and balls of barbed wire.

About two kilometres after **Malé Leváre** the road makes turn towards the March and follows the straightened river Rudava which flows into a deep chasm. One and a half kilometres further, a bridge allows you to cross the river and you will also find a smooth road surface again. Continue the journey with the embankment to the right whereby the road gradually becomes worse. Turn left over the field by Suchohrad until you reach the first buildings. A sign of the Iron Curtain Greenway shows you the way to the centre of town.

## Suchohrad

The community was denied all development perspectives after 1948 which made new constructions and new settlements inadmissible. Visitors required special authorization for the area and the border troops controlled the access roads. Under these conditions, the population sank to half by 1989, which can be seen in the appearance of the town.

## Záhorská Ves

It is not much different in the significantly larger community of Záhorská Ves four kilometres to the south. The varying demands and fate is seen – as in the other towns of the region as well – in the numerous name changes of the town, whereby the Hungarian, Czech, Slovak and German languages play a role. As a "town without development perspectives" such as Suchohrad, the community lost three fifths of the population. Although only a stones throw from the good connection of the Austrian Angern, a reaction ferry was not constructed until 2001, which is to be replaced by a bridge after 2010. Maybe then the future can finally begin. What

a contrast for those who take a detour into the idyllic wine town of Angern!

The quiet road **Stupavská** which leaves the centre of town to the southwest is significantly better to travel on than the one which approaches it from the ferry. It leads through corn and wheat fields until it reaches the edge of the nature reserve Horný les (Oberer Wald).

## Naturschutzgebiets Horný les (Oberer Wald)

This alluvial forest of 543 hectares consists of hard and soft woods, sand dunes as well as tributary rivers and backwaters of the March. You can access it on the dike or along the March. Somewhat further to the south you will find the community of Vysoká pri Morave where the barbed wire of the Iron Curtain literally separated the gardens. Different than the northern neighbours, this town is in the middle of growth. New companies have established themselves here and numerous holiday-goers come here from Bratislava. There are various cultural activities and festivals.

Continue on the **Hlavná** which also continues from the southern edge of town

to the southeast towards Stupava. After five kilometres, cross the straightened river Malina and shortly afterwards turn right where you will have to deal with numerous potholes. In a sharp angle, you will near the railroad embankment and continue parallel thereto. At the most southeast edge of the nature preserve **Dolný les** (Unterer Wald) continue close to the shores of the March. By the small settlement of **Devinske Jazero** a snack bar may be of interest. Shortly afterwards you will see the huge factory grounds of Volkswagen Slovakia to the left and on the right the less modern, but still impressive, long stone bridge which provides the railroad connection between Bratislava and Vienna.

The automobile factory belongs to Devínska Nová Ves which has been a part of Bratislava since the 1970's. In numerous areas it has taken on a city-like character with high rise apartments.

With the Sandberg to the left, continue along the March after the town towards south and you will reach Devín after three kilometres on a wide paved road.

## Devín

*The bright white memorial "Gate to Freedom" with hundreds of engraved names commemorates the deported, expelled and those killed during attempts to flee. The impressive cliff with castle which has been in front of you for several kilometres can not be overseen. The fortification, which was destroyed by Napoleons troops still appears to guard the former Porta Hungarica, the narrow location of the Danube at the merging of the March. The fort, whose Slavic name became German zu Theben, is of meaning for the identity of Slovakia. It was founded in the 9th century during the Great Moravian Empire from which the current states of the Czech Republic and Slovakia originate.*

The route continues on the road to Bratislava. Along the Karlovesky Channel, which cuts a corner of the Danube, you will reach the Lafranconi Bridge. It brings the automotive traffic from the D 2/E 65 to the other side of the Danube, and also – one level lower – the cyclists. The view of the majestic river and the capital is magnificent. Those who continue into the city centre, which you should not miss, will probably take a different bridge.

## Bratislava (Pressburg)

*The only capital in the world that borders on two states is the political, economical and cultural centre of Slovakia and the largest city of the country with a population of 427,000. From the beginning of the 10th century under Hungarian rule, it was the capital of the Hun-*

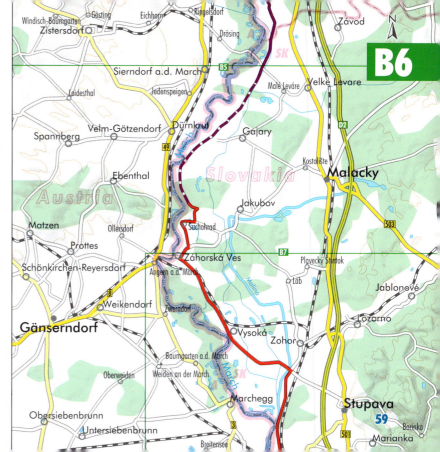

garian Kingdom from 1536, when Hungary was decimated by the Ottomans, until 1848. As such it experienced a period of flourishing which is still evident in the surroundings and the architecture. After relocation of the administration into what is now Budapest, it became the centre of the Slovakian national movement. Capital of the Slovakian constituent state, Bratislava has been the capital of the independent Slovakia since 1993. The area profits from the vicinity to the western European markets. It is developed as a "twin city" together with Vienna, which is 60 kilometres away, and this alone contributes 25 percent of the gross national product. The advantageous location and the high density of universities and research facilities is also due to the settling of numerous global corporations.

Even those who only want to visit the most important historic and modern attractions will not be able to do so in one day. For a first orientation, a small introduction which begins on the Hlavné námestie (Hauptplatz) in the monument protected old town. The most

The castle over Bratislava is the administrative seat

noticeable building is the old City Hall, which is formed by three of the oldest maintained buildings of the city and is decorated with a baroque tower. It now houses the museum of local history. On the opposite, before the Sedlárska ulica (Sattlergasse) you will find the Maximillian fountain, and behind that the noticeable gold decorated Roland palace. The right street corner is dominated by the white Esterházy palace in rococo style and the left by the architecturally similar, but rather more classical infamous Café Mayer. The square is often used for various concerts, festivals and markets.

The Sedlárska leads to the right (NW) towards the Michalská ulica which is lined with street cafés. From a distance of 100 metres, the Michalská brána (Michaeltor) which appears as a baroque church tower greets you from the right, the only maintained medieval city gate. From the view gallery on the sixth floor, you can look over the old town. Right next to the gate you will find the narrowest house in Europe with a width of only 1.30 metres. If you turn to the south, you will reach the great promenade-like Hviezdoslavovo namestie shortly before merging into the road – there you will find the National Theatre and the Germany Embassy – at the crossing with the Panská ulica, through which you will reach the gothic Martinsdom to the right. The meaning of this church for the self confidence of the nation is seen in the reconstruction of the Holy Crown of Hungary which decorates the top of the tower instead of a cross. From 1563 to 1830, this is where the crowning of Hungarian kings took place – which were simultaneously German or Austrian Emperors.

On the other side of the street, which is in front of the church tower, the Židovská ulica runs at the foot of the castle hill. The name refers to the Jewish folk which settled under the protection of the castle during the Middle Ages. A part of the Jewish cemetery has been restored and is curiously found underground in the vicinity of the tram station. The name also reminds of the Jews which were deported in 1939 after the annexation of Austria and of Bohemia and Moravia from the first Slovakian state to Nazi Germany which began south of the Danube at that time.

Idyllic steep alleys and stairs lead up the castle hill. The originally gothic facility with four wings on a cliff 85 metres above the Danube was not of less importance than Devin in the beginning. It was burned down by the French in 1811 after numerous renovations and rebuilt in baroque style after World War II. Its architectural appearance is less spectacular than its position and view.

The city to its feet if influenced by numerous baroque palaces, however also has bold and interesting constructions of the last decades. The Kostol svätej Alžbety (Elisabethkirche) is something special as it is a mixture of traditional and modern styles with it's uniquely formed Hungarian Jugendstil in which pink and blue pastel colours dominate. You will find it in the Bezruova ulica in the south-east of the Old Town.

It need not be mentioned that there is always something happening in such a cultural and popular city. For example, the Bratislava Jazz Days, the Wilsonic Festival (Rock, alternative, pop) and the Bratislava Music Festival (Classical).

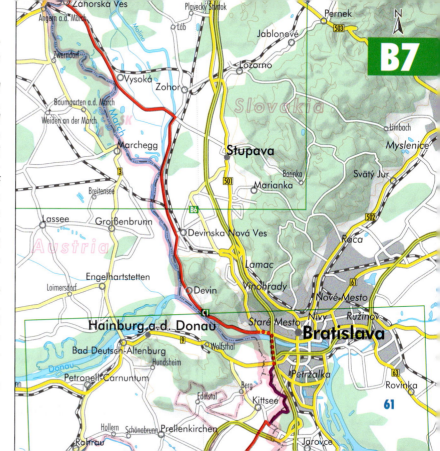

# From Bratislava to Szeged/Horgos                    786 km

## From Bratislava (Slovakia) to the triangle border Austria/Hungary/Slovakia                              55 km

For the continuation to the south, you must take one of the nearby bridges. You must however expect a lot of traffic and less attractive views. The district of Petržalka is one of the largest uniformly built residential areas of Europe with a population of 120,000 in over 40,000 apartments. For those who do not fear the somewhat shorter route through the middle should orient themselves on the Austrian community of Kittsee as next intermediate target. (The Kopianska ulica, which begins to the west of the train station of Petržalka, runs parallel to the railroad tracks and under the autobahn until it reaches the convoy road.) The description of the route is continued from the Lafranconi Bridge.

South of the bridge, a cycle trail runs 2.5 kilometres parallel to the autobahn and then turns to the border crossing Petržalka–Berg. Directly prior to the border the national road must be crossed. Continue on the previous convoy road southeast of the former customs building which follows the border exactly for the next five kilometres. The road is partially lined with trees and in excellent condition up to the border crossing on the southeast edge of Kittsee.

### Kittsee

*Several Croats settled here in the 16th century who had fled from the Turkish invaders. They still maintain their language and culture, however the ethnographic museum in the baroque castle Bathyány on the other side of town has been closed since 2008.*

Continue about 400 metres into the town, then the **Pamastraße** makes a left over the fields and into the community of the same name which also has an active Croatian minority. It is crossed to the left and the direction is kept until **Deutsch Jahrndorf**. At the end of the long village greens, turn right. You should however make a detour straight ahead to the sculpture park of the border triangle. A dirt road leads to the border of Austria, Hungary and Slovenia and from there about 300 metres over the field. To commemorate the fall of the Iron Curtain, various sculptures were created here by international artists in 1989. Memorial stones, border stones and remnants of barbed wire complete the "international symposium" which has become a point of interest for visitors from the three countries.

## The history of Hungary

*The history of Hungary begins far from the national border of today's Hungary. The Magyars, the ancestors of the Hungarians, abandoned their West-Siberian settlement and, after centuries of nomadic existence, finally settled in the territory where the Hungarian Kingdom was formed around 1000 A. D.*

*The Christianised empire however came under Ottoman rule in 1540 and was divided into three sections. The largest part was taken into the Ottoman Empire, the other two became an Ottoman causal state or fell into Austrian territory. Directly after the defeat of the Turks before Vienna, the Habsburg troops conquered* the entire territory. Attempts towards independence were destroyed numerous times until Hungary was made the second main part of the Austro-Hungarian Monarchy in order to reduce the tension in the multiethnic state.

In 1918 Hungary became independent, the democratic government however only lasted a few months and was replaced by a dictatorial conservative regime. Hungary lost large parts of its former territory, including Burgenland, Croatia, Slovakia and Transylvania and saw itself forced to sign the peace agreement in the Grand Trianon of Versailles on June 4, 1920 which confirmed the already existing situation.

In the years between the two World Wars, Hungary increasingly came closer to the German Empire ruled by the Nazis and closed various pacts with them. During World War II, the Hungarian troops actively supported the German campaign in the Balkan and against the Soviet Union, however decided to cooperate with the allies after painful defeats. As a result, the German troops occupied the country and hundred thousand Jews were deported.

Consequently the Red Army conquered Hungary and the capital of Budapest. The hopes of the allies for a democratic constitution were quickly destroyed. In 1949, Hungary received a constitution according to Soviet example, and is a founding member of the Warsaw Pact. The "Hungarian Revolution" was successful in the beginning but put down in 1956. As of 1968, economic reforms took place which were known under the term "Goulash communism". In 1988, a peaceful change of system took place, economic reformers took over the course.

Shortly afterwards, Hungarian border troops began to disassemble parts of the border facilities, due to cost reasons. On June 27, 1989, the Austrian Foreign Minister at the time Alois Mock and his Hungarian counterpart Gyula Horn opened the border fence together.

In August of the same year, a border gate, at the same location, was symbolically opened between Austria and Hungary during the Pan European picnic. On October 23, 1989, the anniversary of the revolution of 1956, the Hungarian Republic was declared a democratic and parliamentary republic and joined NATO and the EU in 2004.

From Jahrndorf continue the tour on the **Nickelsdorfer Straße** over the fields to the southwest. After crossing the Leitha, you will reach **Nickelsdorf**. This community has hosted the rock music festival "Nova Rock" since 2005 which soon became the largest in Austria and led to great traffic problems in the vast surroundings. The

Schulgasse leads to the south and soon becomes the **Lindengasse** and then the **Kleylehofer Straße**. It has a level surface over the autobahn A 4/E 60 to the estate of the same name.

From the bridge you can see the area where the rock concerts take place.

*Local business men initially had big plans for the area between Nickelsdorf and the neighbouring Hungarian Hegyeshalom. A new Las Vegas was planned and an autobahn connection was built on the Hungarian side for this purpose. Then the announced investment sum was reduced to one thirtieth and the original plans for casinos turned into some for a family glitterland. However, today the autobahn exit still ends in the middle of a field.*

*A memorial stone erected in 1961 and a wooden tower commemorate the opening of the Iron Curtain. There is also a memorial in Hegyeshalom which commemorates 60 years of expulsion.*

Before **Kleylehof**, turn right into the cross road and then left after 400 metres. Continue through a forest and again soon over the fields

on a gravel road until you reach **Wittmannshof**. If you continue along the **Schlosspark von Halbturn**, you will soon have pavement under your tires again.

The extensive castle grounds, which are elegant and well maintained, occasionally offer concerts and are also operated by the owners. With a small right-left manoeuvre you will continue in the former direction and soon again reach the fields, which are partly used for cultivating wine. After 7.5 kilometres, Hof Albrechtsfeld in on the left, surrounded by a small forest. The hill behind it offers a couple of covered benches with a nice view.

You will soon reach **Andau**, where the main traffic makes a right. Shortly afterwards you will find the former village green on the left, the centre of which is dominated by the church of St. Nicholas. The combination of baroque and modern elements provided it with two minaret-like round towers. However, what appears to harmonize on the outside is rather unusual on the inside.

The route continues to the southwest. For those who do not shy the detour, you can follow an unusual historical event from here which is connected with the term "Bridge at Andau" and is known in literature and film.

## Bridge at Andau

*The inconspicuous wooden bridge serves the local farmers to reach their fields, which are often on both sides of the embanked Einserkanal and thus also on both sides of the border. In 1956, in the course of the Hungarian revolt, a wave of refugees appeared and one of the last possibilities to reach the west was via this small remote construction. 70,000 people for-*

ged over the bridge until it was destroyed by Hungarian soldiers. 40 years later, a new bridge was erected in collaboration between Hungarian and Austrian soldiers. The location is now marked with an observation tower and visitors are also allowed to enter a limited area on the Hungarian side without formalities.

Along the so-called Fluchtstraße, the nearly nine kilometre long stretch from Andau to the Einserkanal, has been turned into a unique open air gallery with sculptures and installations by numerous artists from around the world.

The journey towards the south begins in the town on the Dammweg, which turns to the left where the triangular Raiffeisenplatz merges into the Ödenburger Straße.

### From Andau (Austria) to Sopron (Hungary)    56 km

A cycle trail accompanies the road from Andau to Tadten. Continue to the right along the village greens and turn left 300 metres further by the yellow chapel. Here you will once again find a cycle trail, although you will once again have to travel on the road before you reach Wallern. The surroundings of this community are influenced by vegetable crops and a row of light greenhouses are not necessarily decorative for the landscape.

The community of **Pamhagen** which soon follows is surrounded by straight wine trellises. The through street continues on the eastern edge of town and crosses the Hauptstraße shortly before you reach

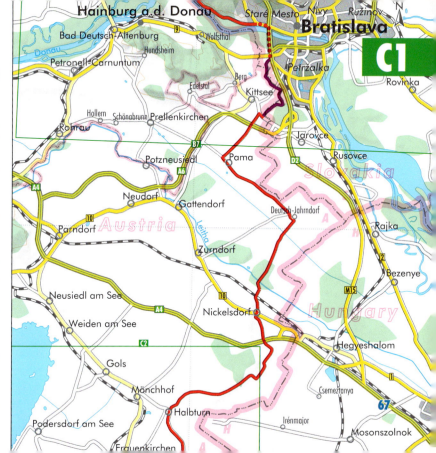

C1

67

the fields again. Here you will see a single standing bell tower on the right at a distance of 300 metres.

It is connected to a historic anecdote and is called the Turk tower by the local people. In the opposite restaurant named thereafter you will find home cooking but also Pannonian treats which taste best sitting outside in the quiet street.

One kilometre from the southern edge of town you will pass the border to Hungary and continue past Nyárliget to Fertőd.

## Fertőd

The name originated 1950 after the Hungarian fert = swamp, is however inseparable with the castle Esterházy and the composer Joseph Haydn for friends of classical music. The entrance into the town is from the northern section of the huge castle grounds so that you near touch the rear of the building before continuing to the right on the Joseph Haydn œt. The "Hungarian Versailles" belongs to the largest rococo castles of Hungary and to the UNESCO World Heritage List. The fact that the reconstruction

View from the former observation tower by Sopron

of the smaller hunting lodge took 46 years is easy to believe considering the extent and furnishings (the middle section can be viewed). The park forms a national park together with the Hanság, the lower moor landscape south of the Neusiedler Lake, which also belongs to the UNESCO World Heritage together with the Austrian national park Neusiedler Lake.

Fertőd continues to the west into the neighbouring community of Fertőszéplak über.

## Fertőszéplak

You will be greeted here by a row of white, gabled buildings in Hungarian peasant

baroque. Several of these attractive arcade houses form the open air folklore museum which is dedicated to the old trades. Adjacent to the double towered All Hallows Church is a baroque Calvary and on the opposite side is the family seat of the noble family Szèchenyi.

The cycle trail around the Neusiedler Lake has been in existence since the visa-free "late socialist" times and has become very popular. It is no wonder that the surrounding communities are well prepared for tourists: For example Hegyk has a thermal spa, well maintained accommodation and numerous dining possibilities.

Continue via **Fertőhomok** and **Hidegség** to Fertőboz, which is known for the "Gloriette" which was built in 1801.

## Fertőboz

A pavilion in round temple style on the top of a hill from which you can enjoy a beautiful view over the lake. You will find the construction to the south of the community after climbing a hill over a few hundred metres.

You will reach **Balf** where the Iron Curtain Trail makes a loop to the north.

Continue towards Fertorákos (Kroisbach) between vineyards and the wetlands of the lake past a high metal border observation tower in the reeds to the right. The long community is a row of points of interest and memorials of various periods.

## Fertőrákos

About 150 metres after the begin of the high building density you will find a small chapel from 1714 to the left at an intersection, close to a new residential building, which has an archaic appearance due to its simple construction and the raw ashlar. The town was part of an Episcopal manor and was protected by a fortification in the Middle Ages. Two massive walls are still maintained and can be found 300 metres further after a slight left curve. Three white statues have been standing in front of it since 1996, one of which is the Madonna of Kroisbach, that form the expulsion memorial from the sculptor Örsi András. It carries the names of the persons expelled fifty years ago. The bishop's palace follows, a stately baroque construction with courtyard on old foundations, surrounded by a well kept garden in French style. On the square on the right side of the street you will find the tourist information. The centre of the square is dominated by the memorial of the public polls of 1921 which resembles a baptistery. The surroundings of Sopron remained part of the Hungarian state due to a referendum.

After the next row of houses, you will find a small square to the left which was turned into a park in 1989. The memorial of the opening of the border consists of a stone block with implied rows of barbed wire. It is split from above with a wedge with the year 1989. In the same area, you will also find the baroque watermill of the Episcopal residence, the facade of which is colourfully decorated and with a sundial. Objects of the miller trade are exhibited in the courtyard. The simple pillory on the narrow village greens once stood as a symbol for jurisdiction above an underground prison. The church, a baroque construction with an old fortifying tower is surrounded by tombstones and columns with artistic styles from baroque to classical.

Upon continuation, you will find memorials to the right: Friedrich von Kreuzpeck, the warhorse from the noble family of Kroisbach is followed by the memorial of World War I and the rescue of Vienna from the Turks with the statue of Holy Trinity, until you reach an old quarry shortly before merging into a crossroad. After centuries of activity, a chasm has been dug here into a hill with a jagged outline and upright cliff walls. On the south side these walls are hollow so that the ceiling stone rests on massive columns – a spectacular setting for the cave theatre, which became well known in Europe since 1970 with musical performances from Wagner and Liszt.

However, with a slight stretch of the imagination, the facilities could also be used as a natural fortress. German officials created a transition and work place here after the annexation of Hungary in 1944, in which thousands of Hungarian Jews and political prisoners were murdered, whereby others were transported to the concentration camps in Germany and Poland. The cavern which served as an execution site still shows numerous bullet holes and has a memorial plaque. Unfortunately, this historical aspect is only seldomly given notice in the German travel literature.

On the northern hill, an over-dimensional piece of barbed wire reaches into the sky. It is the Pan European memorial from Gabriela von Habsburg in order to commemorate the Pan European picnic of 1989, the site of which this route will lead to. It carries a band with the Latin motto of the Pan European Union: In neccessariis unitas in dubiis libertas in omnibus caritas (unity in necessary things; liberty in doubtful things; charity in all things).

**Tip:** In Fertőrákos you will also follow the traces of an antique mystery.

## To Mithraeum                    2 km

In the Roman Empire, the Mithras-cult developed until the 4th century, a mysterious religion which noone was allowed to report about. Because it deviated from the Roman national religion prior to and after the introduction of Christianity, it was mostly worshipped secretly. It was especially common among legionnaires as it only applied to men. A temple of this cult was coincidentally discovered in 1866 under wild vines on the connection road to the neighbouring Austrian community, Mörbisch am See. The restored building is deep underground. This is due to the fact that – Mithras is said to have been born from a stone, which is why he was mainly worshipped in caves. The building can be found directly at the present border crossing. Apart from three altars, is also has a relief of a bull killing which is typical for this cult. This is interpreted astronomically in many ways most prominently: as the end of an era and the beginning of a new powerful one. The Mithraeum from the early third century can be viewed from mid March to mid October. On the 20th anniversary of the Pan European picnic, the 9th symphony from Ludwig van Beethoven was performed here on August 19, 2009.

Memorial of the opened doors

Continue on the cycle trail from Fertorákos to **Mörbisch am See** and turn left after the border onto the paved cycle trail which leads to the site of the Pan European picnic on the road to Sankt Margarethen.

## The Pan European Picnic

On August 19th, the Pan European Union, which was in contact with the opposition of the Eastern Block, held a peace demonstration on the border north of Sopron with the Hungarian Democratic Forum, the Pan European Picnic. During this event, under the patronage of Otto von Habsburg and the Hungarian Minister Imre Pozsgay, a gate was to be symbolically opened in the border fence for one hour.

Many applied to take place in this event, also the GDR refugees in Budapest who thought it would be easier to continue to the west. Thousands had come and when the gate was opened, nearly 700 rushed through to the Austrian side without encountering any resistance worth mentioning. In the following days, the guarding of the borders was increased, but three weeks later, on September 11th, it was opened to GDR citizens without limitations. Next to an educational trail with an observation tower, a row of artworks commemorate the occurrence in various forms of expression including a well house, a freedom bell and the memorial of the opened doors.

## Memorial of the opened doors

On the eastern side you will also find the memorial of the opened doors which commemorates June 27th, when the Hungarian Foreign Minister Gyula Horn cut through the Iron Curtain with his Austrian colleagues. It is clear that this memorial is at the wrong location. There is a serious discussion in Hungary whether it should be relocated to a different location, to Klingenbach.

## Japanese pagoda

On the other side of the street you will find a Japanese pagoda, which was financed by a public initiative as a symbol of the happiness over the reunification of Europe. Cherry trees were planted here as also in numerous locations along the border strip of Berlin. The Japanese celebrate their traditional cherry blossom festival under the flowering cherries. No other plant plays such an important role in the life of the Japanese like the cherry. It is considered a national sanctum, in which one sees a symbol for aesthetic beauty and idealizes the soul of the Japanese knighthood. Unfortunately, the cherry trees have disappeared.

## Memorial "Change"

On August 19, 2009, the 20th anniversary, the memorial "Change" created by Miklós Melocco, which consists of 15 life-size figures with a stylised background, was inaugurated in the presence of the Hungarian President Sólyom, the German Chancellor Merkel and the Austrian Foreign Minister Spindelegger.

**Memorial "Change"**

The educational border trail with informative signs and the integration of the observation tower runs along the Hungarian side of the border. The signposted cycle trail B 31, which leads you to Klingenbach, is on the Austrian side.

After Hungary began with the disassembly of the border protection facilities on May 2, 1989, the Austrian and Hungarian Foreign Ministers symbolically cut through part of the fence by Nickelsdorf on June 27th to emphasize this event.

## Alois Mock and Gyula Horn

June 27, 1989 was a historical day. A quarter of a year before the fall of the wall in Berlin, the Iron Curtain became penetrable. On this day, the Hungarian Foreign Minister Gyula Horn and his Austrian colleague Alois Mock cut through the barbed wire between the two countries.

What brought it about? What was the motivation, especially of the communist government in Hungary? The reasons can be read in a report by János Székely, who became leading commander of the Hungarian border troops in 1986 and was requested to check the electrical border facilities by the Ministry of the Interior in October 1987. For this purpose, he requested a report concerning the conditions from all responsible border commanders. In summary, the electrical signal facilities were out of date in all aspects.

The signal facilities, which were 20 years old at that time, set off alarms for various reasons – only very seldomly due to attempts to flee, usually caused by animals. A protective fence that was erected at a later time was also not able to prevent the false alarms since deer would jump over it. Heavy wind was also one of the more common causes. In total, only ten percent of the alarms were caused by people.

The Hungarian border troops registered an average of 2,000 attempts to flee annually, whereby only ten percent were Hungarian citizens who decided to leave their country via the green border due to spontaneous reasons. Many returned on the day after their escape since 90 percent of the Hungarian population had a passport at that time with which they were allowed to leave the country without problems (so-called "world passport").

The Hungarians were envied for that reason. I will never forget the amazed faces of the GDR participants when in the beginning of the 1980's a Hungarian woman on a canoe tour organised by the Riparian states on the Danube from Ingolstadt to Silistra in Bulgaria told us about her weekend relationship with her boyfriend in England. Every two weeks she would visit him in London and the other weeks he would visit her in Budapest. On this canoe tour, the participants from the GDR were the only ones who were not included in West-Germany and Yugoslavia. For them, the Hungarians lived in a free empire.

The officials also complained about the border facilities in the border areas - also because they would harm the tourism. There were only two alternatives for the Hungarian government: Either completely renew the fence or remove it, whereby the soldiers were to be equipped with modern observation means. The renewing would have cost DM 40 million (€ 20 mio), the removal 7 million (€ 3.5 mio). The Ministry of the Interior took over the position of the border troops and spoke for the removal thereof, whereby the final decision was continuously postponed because it not only affected Hungary but the entire Eastern Block.

After the resignation of János Kádár in May 1988, Imre Pozsgai became the new Minister and there was an initial attempt to remove the border fence on April 18, 1989 in the area of Rayka in the border triangle of Austria, Hungary and Czechoslovakia. On May 3, the removal of the electronic signal facilities by the border troops was declared at an international press conference. On May 28th, half of the facilities were already removed, the Hungarian government officially agreed to it. At the same time, the military troops were ordered to help with the removal which is why the electrical facilities were already completely removed by September.

On August 19th, the so-called "Pan European picnic" took place that Otto von Habsburg and Imre Pozsgai organised. 700 GDR citizens used the opportunity to flee. On September 11th, the border between Hungary and Austria was opened. Since 25,000 GDR citizens used this possibility to flee within the following three weeks, the GDR government prohibited travels to Hungary.

June 27, 1989 had a prelude and an aftermath – was however also a grand performance **73** itself. Namely when the two Foreign Ministers Gyula Horn and Alois Mock wanted to cut through the Iron Curtain in a festive act by Soporn, the previously removed fence had to be put up again.

From Klingenbach continue over **Baumgarten** past a radar station until you reach Schattendorf whereby a small part of the stretch in the forest is not paved.

## Shots from Schattendorf

The shots from Schattendorf are considered the beginning of the end of the First Austrian Republic. In 1927 Austria was characterised by conflicts between the Christian socialists, social democrats, German nationalists and their para-military organizations. Violent conflicts between right wing extremists and social democrats were every day events.

When demonstrations of unarmed socialist Schutzbund members took place on January 30, 1927 in Schattendorf, three nationalist combatants opened fire with their shotguns. Five people were injured. The seven year old Josef Grössing

*"Pointer" at the rest stop by Schattendorf*

from Schattendorf and the 41 year old war veteran Matthias Csmarits from Klingenbach were killed.

The offenders appeared before court in Vienna on July 5, 1927, were however released again nine days later due to alleged self defence. As a result, on July 15, the day after the verdict, socialist workers marched from the outer areas of Vienna into the city. By parliament and the university, mounted police went against the demonstrators with pulled swords. There were massive street fights and the palace of justice was set in flames. The riots were ended violently. The result: 80 dead and 800 injured.

The gap continued to grow and ended with the self dissolution of the parliament, the prohibiting of social democracy and the civil war in February 1934.

In Schattendorf continue on the **Koglweg** (B 30) to the church and past the cemetery towards Agfalva. After crossing the border, the trail is no longer paved. Keep to the right and after crossing the railroad tracks you will reach Agfalva on a paved road. Turn left there and continue on the cycle trail adjacent to the road through the town and turn right in the left curve. Continue over the river and remain on the southern side of the railroad tracks which is unfortunately not signposted. After one kilometre you will reach the paved cycle trail to the train station in Sopron. Trains depart from here travelling directly to Vienna and Budapest.

## Sopron (Ödenburg)

The exposed position in respect of the western European states, once a massive disadvantage, has become one of the most important factors for the economic upswing. In the polls of 1921, the city voted for Hungary with more than 62 percent, is however officially bilingual. During the Roman Empire it played an important role as border station on the Amber Road in the province of Pannonia. After a devastating fire in 1676 it was rebuilt in baroque style and the old town is still influenced thereby today. Nice alleys, architectural rarities from gothic to baroque, numerous memorials, wine cellars with a village feeling, but also music programs and shopping possibilities make the town with a population of 55,000 also attractive for tourists and investors. After Budapest, you will find the most historic buildings of Hungary here which is why the city has served as a filming site numerous times.

The landmark of Sopron is the 61 metre high Fire Tower, which houses an exhibition concerning the history of the city in the upper levels. Since the 13th century it has formed the northern gate tower. It received its current form with the baroque helmet and the surrounding balcony after the fire. On the southern side, the "Gate of Faith" was installed to commemorate the public poll. Since then the town has carried the title "civitas fidelissima", very faithful city.

Triangle border

The city hall near the main square is an eclectic building from 1896 which is very impressive. On the opposite corner you will find the Storno House, one of the most beautiful buildings in the city. It has two elaborately decorated balconies over two levels. On the main square you will also find the apothecary museum in number 2 and in number 6, the Fabricius House with stone memories of the Roman times including a marble tomb and the original altar relief from the Temple of Mithras in Fertorákos. The south side of the square is dominated by the tower of the Goat Church, where crowning of monarchs takes place

and meetings of parliament. It has fresco masterpieces. The street follows the medieval fortification of the city and is therefore called the "Grabenrunde"(Ditch Turn). The fountain of faith symbolise three events of great meaning: the progression to a free kingdom in 1277 after resisting Bohemian occupation, the public polls of 1921 and the opening of the border in 1989.

To the southwest, the òj utca branches off from the main square. In number 1 you can view the remnants of the Roman forum and in number 22 you can view the gothic synagogue, which is unique to Middle Europe. It was restored in 1967 and has a Mikwe, the ritual bath. The old town is surrounded by massive parts of the city wall, especially in the west and east, where you can take a rest.

**From Sopron to Szentgotthard**          **135 km**

The **Magyar út** leads to the south and further the **Kszegi út** which goes slightly uphill after the railroad tracks to **Harka**. The new, small border crossing makes the further continuation to Austria possible, however only on a sandy road. Informative plaques show what the border area looked like in the past. The following town of Neckenmarkt is known for its traditional flag swinging.

## Neckenmarkt

*The flag was originally a symbol of thanks for the support in the successful battle by Lackenbach against the Turks in 1620. The Sunday after Corpus Christi is the day of the flag and the boys of town demonstrate their strength and skills in numerous parades.*

In the adjacent **Horitschon** you will meet the B 62 (Hauptstraße) and follow it for 100 metres to the left until you reach a fork in the road where you once again turn towards the south (**Günser Straße**). Before you reach **Großwarasdorf** the road takes you downhill in large curves. Continue several hundred metres through the town which is 81.5 % populated by Croats from the Burgenland (the German speaking population is about 15 percent). Where the Hauptstraße makes a large right curve – the former pillory was robbed of its

actual character – turn left (**Kirchenberg**) and continue straight ahead where the road merges after the right curve (**Schulstraße**). The route through the town is signposted towards Nebersdorf and Lutzmannsburg.

## Nebersdorf

*The castle of Nebersdorf is a typical example of a noble west Hungarian residence, as they were created after the wars with the Turks. The side wings appear very modest, the middle section disproportioned, which is emphasised by the interesting but far too large portico on the garden side. The facilities were purchased by the municipality in 1952, the trees in the park cut down and turned into parcels for residential buildings. A private owner has unsuccessfully attempted to utilize the building in a profitable manner since then.*

Continue through **Croatian Geresdorf**, where you will be greeted in two languages,

Plaque on the educational trail

to Lutzmannsburg which lies on the border.

## Lutzmannsburg

*The old town was formerly on the Rabnitz but was rebuilt at a higher position after the floods at the beginning of the 19th century. A small settlement remained next to the catholic church, which uses the elevated area of the former administrative building. The traditional winegrowing area has the highest temperatures and the most hours of sunshine* in Austria, but suffered from the separation from the neighbouring country and lost half of the population due to emigration. The opening of the thermal spa in 1994, which has been expanded three times since then, has had a stabilising effect: The once agricultural village has become one of the largest areas of tourism in the Burgenland.

*In order to maintain this success, the people refuse to allow lorries to cross the border even* though the Hungarian neighbouring village has provided a complete street: Namely, the one directly adjacent to the relaxation area of the thermal spa and the hotel. Since it is not possible to continuously resist the pressure of the neighbours and the regulations of the Schengen Agreement, which demand that all border crossings must be free at all possible locations, a connection road will eventually be built.

Continue over the village greens with the classical Evangelic church – a rarity in catholic Austria – towards the border in the east. Zsira is on the Hungarian side and hides a treasure in the middle: the well balance castle of the family Rimanóczy from 1730 which – how much longer? – is used as a retirement home.

At the end of town, turn right towards Répcevis, where the last refugee who tried to overcome the Iron Curtain was shot.

## Kurt-Werner Schulz

With his wife and 6 year-old son Johannes, the 36 year old Kurt-Werner Schulz wanted to flee to Austria on August 22, 1989. They had already crossed over the destroyed border fence when the border soldier tried to arrest him. His wife and son continued to run. Kurt-Werner Schulz resisted and was shot at the smallest distance during a hand fight and was killed. It could be seen from the tracks that the victim was dragged from Austrian territory into Hungary. The fact-finding committee confirmed the border violation by two Hungarian border soldiers.

Whether it had been intended or an accident could not be determined.

20 years later, the border soldier who was 20 at that time stated (Die Presse, 14.08.09): "He simply let the woman and child run. But he attempted to stop the man. It was probably bad luck that there was a second soldier nearby. He obviously felt the pressure to do something. If he had been alone..."

Unfortunately there is no commemorative cross for the last refugee who was shot while attempting to overcome the Iron Curtain.

Continue downhill from Répcevis to **Peresznye**. You will need to use more energy to **Horvátzsidány** and also afterwards before continuing through a forest and then on to Kőszeg (Güns).

## Kőszeg

The "jewelry box of Hungary" is in great distress. After the collapse of the for the region once very important textile industry, the community is now attempting to establish itself in tourism. The conditions therefore are good since the geographic location offers good

Hungary and the EU

recreational and winter sport possibilities. In the Kőszeg Mountains, an extension of the Alps, there is a varied and original selection of species as well as educational trails, hiking trails and museums in the Austro-Hungarian National Park.

The architecture of the town with a population of 12,000 is mainly that of Habsburg from the 18th century. Those beginning with the tour at the F tér (Main square) are however on the younger ground since this district on the southern edge of the old town was built at the end of the 19th century. This also applies to the impressive Herz-Jesu Kirche

with the colourful glass windows. The large Gate of Heroes is another historical monument, which is worth visiting.

Since 1932 it commemorates the successful defence of the city during the third wave of the Turkish Wars 400 years before. After 19 attempts, the last attackers retreated at 11:00. Since 1777 the church bells ring daily at this time for this reason. The Gate of Heroes is on the grounds of the southern city gate, the most important access to the city.

The actual market square is the smaller and also narrower Jurisics tér, named after the Croatian general who is to be thanked for the retreat of the Turkish attackers. To the left you will see the city hall, which is still in use, with the facade from 1597. Also interesting is the two-story apothecary museum Zum Goldenen Einhorn a little further in number 11. The old houses appear too low since the area was elevated with a layer of rubble after several devastating fires. In the middle you will see two similar churches which appear to be rivals, which they once were. When the German Lutherans became stronger after 1558, the Calvinists banned them from using the Jacob's Church. They built a church adjacent thereto – smaller but with a higher tower. The church soon fell into catholic hands after the counter-reformation. This also affected the gothic Jacob's Church which received numerous baroque attachments over time. In 1937, wall paintings were found in the southern side nave from the time of construction.

The former Esterházy castle is accessible from the Rajnis utca, which was named after Miklós Jurisics (Nikola Juriši) since 1932 as well as the market square. A bridge leads you over the moat and into the castle, which received it's current appearance in 1777 after the devastating fire.

On the other side of the eastern ring of the old town you will find the ruins of a large synagogue on the Kiss János utca. The Jews of Kőszeg were the last to be deported to Auschwitz in 1944. In the work camp, 4,500 people died of typhus. The 2,000 who survived were forced to a death march over the Alps to the concentration camp Ebensee before the Soviet Army arrived.

From the train station you can travel directly to Szombathely where you can continue travel in many directions.

Leave the town to the southwest towards Bozsok (Rohonci utca). Vineyards accompany the quiet road to Kőszegszerdahely.

## Kőszegszerdahely

This and the surrounding villages are known for discoveries of Celtic and Roman settlement remains.

## Bozsok

Bozsok is very close to the Austrian border. It once belonged to the family Sibrik, which divided their property into two areas in 1552. As a result, two castles were built in the village. The older of the two is still maintained on the northern edge of the village and serves as a hotel. The Batthyány family took over the southern castle which is now a ruins – similar to the former Church of Holy Trinity.

Follow the Dorfstraße, which gradually turns to the south, along the border to **Bucsu** and further under the highway (89). Make a right turn afterwards towards **Narda** and **Felscsatar**. You will come to a fork in the road at the beginning of town. Straight ahead leads you to the lower part of town, **Alsócsatár**, which lies next to a river, and to the left the somewhat wider road leads to the upper Flescsatar.

## Felsőcsatar

An enthusiastic resident created a private border museum here which comprises an observation tower, restriction facilities and information plaques. The main focus lies on the mine fields

Observation tower on the border

and the spring guns. The friendly operator performs the tours himself and is able to make himself understood in German as well. The facilities are well signposted with the term "vasfüggöny múzeum".

Continue to the south via **Vaskeresztes** and **Horvátlöv** until you reach Pornóapáti (until 1899 Pornó, Pernau).

## Pornóapáti

The founding of the city dates back to the 13th century and is connected with an abbey (apáti). This was destroyed during the Turkish wars and was rebuilt with increased reinforcements. It was however destroyed again and a

manor was built on the site which now also lies in ruins to the west of the town. Here the Hungarian border forms a protrusion into the Austrian Burgenland. This, together with the fact that the official border stations were far away provided a fairly good possibility for GDR citizens to cross the "green" border on foot in the summer and autumn of 1989. Many abandoned cars were found in the forests to the northwest.

The irregular course of the border causes you to cross the border several times in a short period on the further journey to the south. It begins with the journey to **Bildein** (AT), which is connected by a newly paved road. Once you have passed **Eberau** with the large moated castle from 1400, you will reach **Szentpéterfa** (HU), the population of which is 80 % Croatian. A newly constructed road leads to the south into Austria's **Moschendorf** which was destroyed three times during the Turkish wars.

## Moschendorf

The creation of the Burgenland lead to the result that in 1921 the community was surrounded by the border on three sides. It is no wonder that, in the years from 1930 to 1938, several citizens emigrated to the USA due to the economic crisis. The history of the village reports that currently more Moschendorf citizens live overseas than locally.

Continue to the west in **Pinkamindszent** towards Strem and cross the border once again. You will come to the road which leads you to Heiligenbrunn, an old wine town.

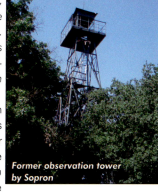
*Former observation tower by Sopron*

## Heiligenbrunn

It is known for its cellar district where you will find 140 cellar houses, half of them covered with straw, from the 16th and 17th centuries. Two of them have exhibitions. No question that you can also enjoy the wine at numerous tables under the trees.

You will have a hill to conquer after **Reinersdorf**. The hills also continue through **Großmürbisch** to **Unterberg** by Kleinmür-

bisch where you turn left and continue downhill to **Inzenhof**. After a right curve, the road continues through the town and two kilometres after the constructions, turn left onto the 319. After four and a half kilometres you will reach **Heiligkreuz** whereby one section has an eleven percent grade which is a great burden for man and material.

Once you have reached the village, turn left into the **Untere Haupstraße** and soon afterwards right into the **Marktstraße**. On the left you will find the guest house Karoline Pummer, which offers food and overnight accommodation (not the be confused with the much larger guest house Rudolf Pummer in the Obere Hauptstraße). Continue the journey on this smaller road which is called the **St. Gotthardter Straße** after the left curve and leads over the fields into the industrial area of **Neuheiligenk-**

reuz. Keep to the left at the power plant and then cross the border straight ahead on a small bridge. To the right, behind the Raab, lies Szentgotthárd, the centre of the Slovenian minority of Hungary.

## Szentgotthárd

The name and founding of the town goes back to the Cistercian monastery of 1183. The monastery which was constructed as a fortification with moat was destroyed in 1605 and the courtyard is now the largest public park in the city. After their return, the Cistercians built the baroque church around 1750 which is the third largest in Hungary and dominates the appearance of the city. The new monastery was dissolved in 1950.

The economic upswing came with the opening of the railroad line which continued until the demarcation of 1821. The loss of the hinterland due to the Iron Curtain had a bad influence on the economy of the area. Since the opening of the border and becoming a member of the EU, the course has changed.

The industrial park to the north is operated together with Heiligenkreuz and a thermal spa should attract visitors in the future. There are direct connections from the train station to Graz and Sombathely.

**From Szentgotthárd to Nagykanizsa     120 km**

From the main square, continue straight ahead towards the south on the **Árpád-Straße** and out of town. Again follow the stretch surrounded by trees down an eleven percent grade, then uphill again and before you reach **Apátistvánfalva** you will be rewarded with a further downhill stretch. The somewhat higher church gives the town a sense of tranquillity. A little later you will pass the border to Slovenia without formalities.

## The history of Slovenia

The border to Slovenia was formed in the 15th century under the rule of the Austrian Habsburgs. During the ruling period of Empress Maria Theresa (1740-1780) the region experienced an economic upswing. The general compulsory education with Slovenian lessons was introduced for the first school years. Her son, Emperor Joseph II, did away with serfdom and provided everyone the right to freedom of religion. In 1797, the first Slovenian newspaper was published.

The revolution of 1848/49 also moved the Slovenian intellectuals, first demands of Slovenian autonomy became loud. The merging of all south-Slavic people in the federation within the K and K Empire was openly propagated.

During World War I, the Slovenes fought on the side of the Austro-Hungarians. After the collapse of the Habsburg Empire, the Kingdom of Serbia, Croatia and Slovenia was proclaimed on December 1, 1918, which was called the Kingdom of Yugoslavia as of 1929. Within Yugoslavia, the Slovenes were granted their own administration. However, they had to transfer areas to Italy in the border contract from Rapallo.

During World War II Slovenia, as a part of Yugoslavia, was attacked, occupied and separated by the Germans, Italians and Hungarians in April 1941. A Slovenian communist liberation front, the Osvobodilna Fronta (OF), was founded.

From 1945 to 1990, Slovenia was a socialist constituent republic which belonged to the Yugoslavian Federation with the right of succession. In accordance with the Paris Peace Conference, a part of the coastal region was returned to Slovenia in 1947 and after the London Agreement of 1954 also the southern part of Trieste, exclusive of the city of Trieste. Slovenia strengthened its national and educational facilities in socialist Yugoslavia, later also its economic independence.

After the ten day conflict with the Yugoslavian army in 1991 and the collapse of Yugoslavia, Slovenia became a sovereign and democratic state. On May

1, 2004, it became a member of the European Union and has been a member of the European Monetary Union since January 1, 2007.

The widely scattered community of **Čepinci** welcomes you with further downhill grades and curvy stretches, but also with the Linden-Bar (Lipa) where you can take a break. Pass Markovci, which is known for its carnival figures and continue to the southeast until you reach **Šalovci**. Turn right here onto the 232 and after 300 metres turn left over the railroad tracks. The road continues slightly uphill between the fields and then becomes a forested area with numerous curves.

You will reach **Domanjševci**, continue through town to the left and then leave town again to the right on the 724. Continue to **Pordašinci** via **Ivanjševci**, **Berkovci** and **Prosenjakovci**, where you will find an old wooden church. The next points of orientation are **Motvarjevci** and **Kobilje** and then you have to change directions for the next five and a half kilometres: **Dobrovnik** lies to the southeast, a wine growing area with a higher number of Hungarian residents than Slovenian. The 442 connects to the roundabout where you continue your original direction to the left. The communities of **Kamovci** and **Mostje** follow. Afterwards you will come to a roundabout on the north-western road of **Dolga vas**. Continue in the same direction and through the vineyards of the town, which has a guesthouse/hotel.

**Tip:** You should take a 300 metre detour to the left where

you will find the very well maintained Jewish cemetery of Lendava, the only one in the region which remained unharmed. It is not highly visited any more – as proven by the missing gravestones – but it is an oasis of peace and cultural history.

After Lendava there are always buildings in sight along the route.

## Lendava

*42 percent of the eastern community at the tip of Slovenia is Hungarian speaking. In the transit stations for petrol and crude oil pipelines, important chemical and petrochemical companies have developed.*

*The castle is important for the appearance of the town which is not impressive due to its beauty but its size at an elevated level. It houses a museum with various exhibitions including one of the late Bronze Age since the western Pannonian area is rich on findings from this period.*

*On the opposite side of this narrow and long community you will find the unusual cultural house of the famous Hungarian architect Imre Makovecz. He mainly used natural materials* and in the design he incorporated elements from the history and mythology of the town. This created a detailed ensemble which occasionally reminds of Antoni Gaudi. The building is used for theatre, musical and dance events, but also for conferences and – together with other towns – also for the yearly doll festival in summer.

*The market square is dominated by the two imperial roofs of the church of St. Katherine, which has an attractive baroque pulpit. On the opposite side you can have a cup of coffee in the Gostina Kancal and a bicycle store is adjacent thereto. Not far away, one of the two synagogues existing in Slovenia was restored and is today used for exhibitions and events.*

Continue straight ahead through town and then seven kilometres along vineyards until you reach **Pince**. Shortly afterwards you will find yourself in Hungary again. Here Budapest is planned to be connected with Graz and Ljubljana and from the border to the next target of Nagykanizsa you will be accompanied by a new autobahn.

You will reach **Csörnyeföld** via **Tornyiszentmiklós** and **Dobri** while passing fields and vineyards. The region to the right partially belongs to the flood area of the Mura and in **Murarátka** the roads squeeze between the hills and the curves of the Mura.

In Letenye, which has been an important border crossing to Croatia since 1923, the landscape is again somewhat more open.

## Letenye

*This is where aromatic, fresh white wines originate which can be tasted in several old cellars. After numerous pillages by Turkish troops and a loss of population due to the plague, the town lost its status as a market township and did not experience an upswing until the 1930's. In 1989 it was declared a city.*

Turn right at the church and again left after 800 metres (**Petfi Sándor utca**) towards Murakereszetúr. The initially bumpy road leads over the autobahn towards **Tótszerdahely** and **Molnári** where you turn left after the attractive little church and follow the sign towards Nagykanizsa (13 km). The following community of **Semjénháza** lies somewhat elevated and **Szepetnek** even has a reservoir. Continue slightly downhill towards **Kiskanizsa** and then to **Nagykanizsa**.

**Tip:** There are direct connections from the train station to Zagreb and Budapest.

### *Von Nagykanizsa to Barcs*      **85 km**

Follow the **Csengery út** to the south on the eastern side of the train station. You will soon pass Miklósfa and continue through the fields and a hilly forest area until you reach **Surd**. A good kilometre after the constructions, continue between the fields to the left in a large zigzag until you reach **Somogybükkösd**. Turn right here and follow the gentle ups and downs towards

**Porrogszentpál** which turns into a serpentine like ascend before you reach **Porrog**. **Porrogszentkirály** follows and afterwards you will reach the somewhat more travelled road to Csurgó.

### Csurgó

*This community with a population of 6,000 is mainly known as a historical educational centre of the Reformed Church of Hungary. Shortly after entering the town you will see the white Catholic Church of the Holy Ghost, where you turn right. The solid tower from the 13th century is the remainder of a castle of the Knights Templar. During the Turkish period the church was used as a mosque and later renovated in the baroque style.*

*A good kilometre further south you will find the unique Reformed Church which pre-*

sents a successful combination of traditional and modern with its three tower construction. The building opposite with the ridge turret is a museum which was created in 1975. Further south on the right you will find the new parish hall with modern architecture that incorporates many natural materials. The city hall on the opposite side appears stately in comparison thereto. On the rear side, a nice park invites you to take a rest.

This naturally also applies to the much larger park on the opposite side, right next to the parish hall. A 100 metre long narrow alley leads to a building similar to a castle. It is the Calvinistic Gymnasium, which was founded in 1794 by Count Festetics. It was transformed into the first national educational establishment for teachers in 1869 and received the current building in 1896. The establishment, which also comprises a valuable library, is named after the patriotic Hungarian poet Mihály Csokonai Vitéz, who was employed here for one year in 1799 as a supply teacher.

**Tip: There are direct connections from the** train station to Dombovar and Gyekenyes.

The road continues through fields, small plantations and nurseries to **Berzence**, over which a large hunting seat of the family Festetics thrones. Pass the church and turn right shortly before the end of town towards Barcs. After **Somogyudvarhely** continue through the fields. On the right side you will already find bayous of the Drava (Drau). This indicates a level landscape and the journey to **Bélavár** is comfortable. This community has access to an idyllic bayou of the river and in the following town of **Vizvár** you will reach the main stream. The community of **Heresznye**, which lies downstream, is separated from the Auwald by a small piece of Croatia which reaches over the river. Here you will find a nice view of the gravel banks and cliffs of the river. Continue to Babócsa via **Bolhó**, which has a large number of stores and restaurants.

## Babócsa

Although the town has many things to offer, it has yet to have sustained success with tourists. Officially people complaining about a very high level of unemployment and the burden connected with a large number of Roma settlements. The community experienced its best times several centuries ago when the Turks occupied the castle in 1555 for a good 100 years and created an administration. At the beginning of the 19th century, the citizens took over the area. Several castles provide evidence of this period. Stores, restaurants and guest houses have been established around the large green Szabadság tér (Freedom square), the former market place.

On the road which then makes a right, you will find a second building complex. This is the castle of the Somssich family. You will find a second parallel road which leads away from the through street and to the Turkish well house from the 18th century, which however may have been reconstructed in the 19th century. A little further ahead on the left you will find the diagonal castle which belonged to Meresz. It now serves as a museum and is surrounded by an English garden. The thermal spa lies to the south, left over from the search for oil and gas in 1953 which was rewarded with a large

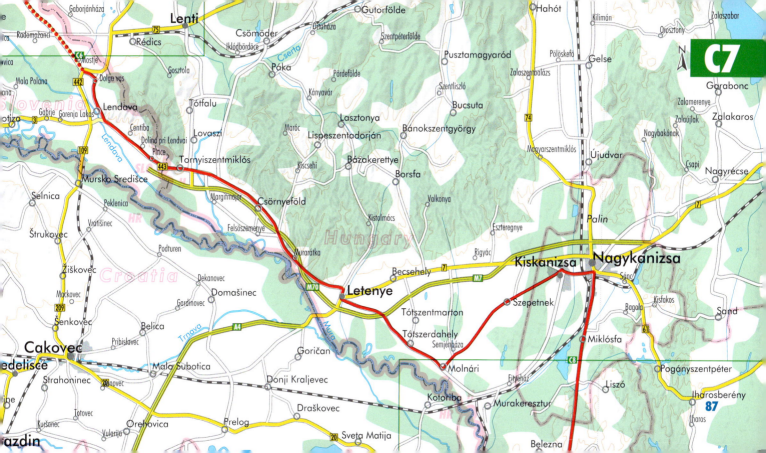

natural gas field.

Continue through the town, over the stream Rinya and after 400 metres you will find the attraction for which Babócsa is actually known on the left: a meadow of twelve hectares covers the area which once was occupied by a Turkish village.

## Basa-kert

In spring and early summer it is an ocean of various daffodils which is celebrated with its own festival every year. Apart from the beauty of Basa-kert (Garden of pasha), the actual treasure lies below the surface. Apart from the now revealed foundation of a Benedictine monastery, archaeologists also found a stately manor, a seraglio, a Turkish steam-bath, large amounts of household items and even a Turkish road. Opposite the daffodil field, turn right at the roundabout towards Drávaszentes via Komlósd. There you will find the modern educational and visitor centre of the Danube-Drau National Park, which is an interesting sight with its organic forms and natural construction materials. Small

**Barcs – before the border to Croatia**

groups can spend the night here.

After a further five kilometres you will reach the new centre of Barcs.

## Barcs

The city with a population of 12,000 does not have the character of a city. Nevertheless, the city is changing fast despite the negative influences since 1989. For example, the main industry of construction collapsed in the 1990's. Additionally the poorly performed privatisation created large problems in the agriculture which lead to a necessary reduction of livestock to a level of personal

needs. For more than 50 years the Agricultural Production Cooperative (LPG) was the largest employer. The current unemployment rate lies at 19 percent.

On the other hand, a new city centre and shopping mile were built in 1994, which provide visitors and locals alike with shopping and recreational facilities. The Polus Shopping Centre targets the buying-power of the nearly 130,000 Croatian tourists. The shopping possibilities are still to be expanded. Ironically, the new centre is similar to an outdoor market, although better maintained and arranged. An additional colourful market with travelling dealers belongs to the concept.

The possibilities that the national park offers are also planned to be expanded. Apart from the nature-tourism this includes water sports and boat tours, which require corresponding infrastructures. Furthermore, there are still many possibilities with the surrounding thermal springs.

There are direct connections from the train station to Szentiörinc and Gyekenyes.

## From Barcs (Hungary) to Donji Miholjac (Croatia) — 100 km

The route to Croatia is signposted. The controlled border crossing lies before the bridge over the Drava. Here you will have to present your passport. On the opposite side, you will pass through the town of **Terezino Polje**. Continue a further four kilometres on the E 661 until you find yourself in the middle of the town of **Gornje Bazje** where you turn left in a right curve. The quiet route leads through the fields to **Veliko Polje** where you turn left and after 500 metres to the right again. About 400 metres before the end of the constructions, a sand and gravel road branches to the right. After two kilometres you will reach **Žlebina**. There are piles of corn in the yards: Those seeking an idyllic location will find what they are looking for. Where the through street merges with a cross-road, turn right and you will reach **Rušani**. Continue on this road and after a few kilometres you will reach the town of

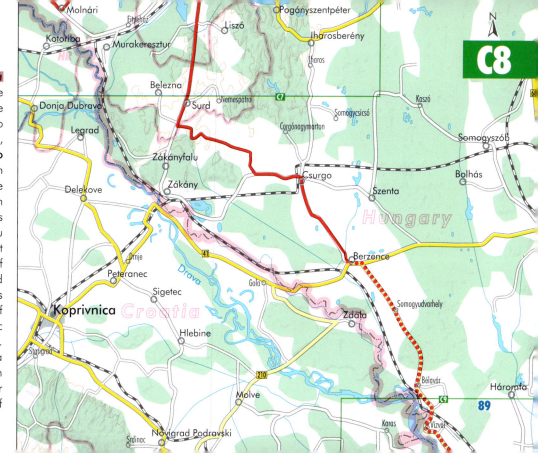

**Gradina** which is located at three former bayous of the Drau. The town has a population of 4,500 but appears smaller as it is quite spread out. However, you will find a post office, a store and not less than three bakeries at one crossing.

## The history of Croatia

In 879, Duke Branimir was addressed as "dux Croatorum" by Pope John VIII, thereby recognizing him as the ruler of Croatia. Duke Tomislav reigned from 910 to 928 and was crowned the first King of Croatia around 925.

With the crowning of the Hungarian King Koloman to King of Croatia in Biograd by Zadar in the year 1102, Croatia became a member of the Personal Union with Hungary through an agreement (Pacta conventa). It existed in various forms with several interruptions until 1918.

In the middle of the 15th century, large areas of Hungary and Croatia fell under the rule of the Ottoman Empire (1451-1699). After the Napoleonic Wars, several areas of Croatia fell under Austrian rule in 1815 while others, such

Barcs

as the Kingdom of Croatia and Slavonia were ruled by Hungary. In the second half of the 19th century, the desire for more independent rights grew among the Croatian population.

After World War I, Croatia began to separate itself from the Austro-Hungarian monarchy. As a result, the Croatian area along the eastern shores of the Adriatic Sea was occupied by Italy, the annexation thereof was approved in 1915 in the London Agreement. At the end of 1918, the Kingdom of Serbia, Croatia and Slovenia was formed. Many Croats rejected the monarchy, felt at a disadvantage and demanded that Croatia becomes a republic.

The constitution proposed a central organisation of the state which assured predominance to the Serbs, as the largest de facto population. In 1929, King Aleksandar I abolished the parliament and renamed the country the Kingdom of Yugoslavia. He ruled as a dictator mainly with the help of Serbian officers. As a result, Ante Paveli founded the Ustaša movement which was supported by Mussolini.

After Germany's attack on the Kingdom of Yugoslavia, it surrendered to the Axis Powers on April 17, 1941. Croatia became a German vassal state. With the support of the Axis Powers, Ante Paveli proclaimed the Independent State of Croatia (NDH) on April 10th and declared himself head of state. He created a fascist dictatorship which systematically followed and killed the Jews, Serbians, Romanies, Croatian anti-Fascists and others. The concentration camp Jasenovac sadly became known which also went down in history as the Croatian Auschwitz.

An armed protest of the Croatian communists against the Ustaša Regime began in the summer of 1941 which controlled large areas of the country in 1942 and 1943. Apart from Tito, Andrija Hebrang was one of the leading personalities.

After the end of the war, Croatia became one of the six constituent republics in socialist Yugoslavia under Tito. After the death of Tito in 1980, the tension increased between Croatia and the Yugoslavian administration dominated by Serbs. At the end of the 1980's, the striving towards more autonomy had turned into the demand for independence. The Croat Franjo Tuman, who had fought against the Ustaša Regime on Tito's side, received great encouragement from the Croatian population.

After the weakened Yugoslavian administration had agreed to a multi-party system, Tuman founded the Croatian Democratic Union (HDZ) in 1990. It soon took on the character of a People's Party, received the majority of the votes in the election of the seats of parliament and elected Tuman as president.

After a referendum concerning the independence of Croatia, which more than 90 % of the population participated in, 93.2 % voted for

sovereignty. Croatia declared independence in June of 1991 under Franjo Tuman, which was recognised internationally.

The Yugoslavian People's Army which was dominated by Serbs attempted to crush their striving towards independence under the rule of Milosevic. The Croatian War which lasted nearly four years did not end until after the military success of the Croats and with the Dayton Agreement at the end of 1995. Croatia is an official member of the EU since June 18, 2004.

Follow the road until after you pass the church and turn left into the straight and narrow road to Suhopolje via **Lipovac**.

## Suhopolje

The town founded by Croats and Germans has a population of about 8,000 which is distributed over 23 villages of the surroundings. The town forms the economical and cultural centre of the villages. The temple-like classical church cannot be overseen. It does not appear to belong in a village with its balanced proportions of gleaming white. The castle was built at the end of the 18th century and lies in the part on the southwest side of the street. Although abandoned and significantly battered, it appears that it could still be renovated. Trains travel directly to Zagreb and Koprivinica from the train station.

Continue to the northeast towards Orešac.

## Orešac

Although the streets are rather quiet here, the people are lively and active. As is common for outlying settlements, the "exotic" cyclist is often greeted with a friendly wave.

On the way to **Novaki** you will find a few wet forest areas, but then the landscape is again mainly agricultural. The next intermediate targets are **Vaškaš**, **Kapinci** and **Sopje** which is also the end of the long, straight sections for a while. You are very close to the Drau again and some of the following towns have moved in between the bayous. This also applies for Sopje, which took over the administration of the surrounding villages, as well as for **Gornje Predijevo** and **Noskovci**.

You will move away from the river again when you continue towards Cadavica. At the beginning of town you will meet the 34, which you will follow for the next 50 kilometres. It is more heavily travelled than the last sections, but unfortunately there is no alternative. It first makes a curve through **Cadavica** where you will find a church reconstructed in baroque with a belfry. The oldest Slavic remains of Croatia were revealed to the south of here (6th-7th century).

Continue straight ahead for the next ten kilometres until you change directions after passing through the town of **Podravska Moslavina**, which is due to the position of a curve in the Drau. After **Viljevo**, which you will pass on the northern side, you will be about 50 metres from the river and have a nice view of its course over several kilometres. A little later you will reach Donji Miholjac.

## Donji Miholjac

The city with a population of 10,000 offers overnight accommodation, for example in the three-star Hotel Slavona, and shopping possibilities. Illyrian tribes, Romans and Awarians settled at this location. Croats have also been here for more than 1,000 years. The name is in connection with the Church of St. Michael.

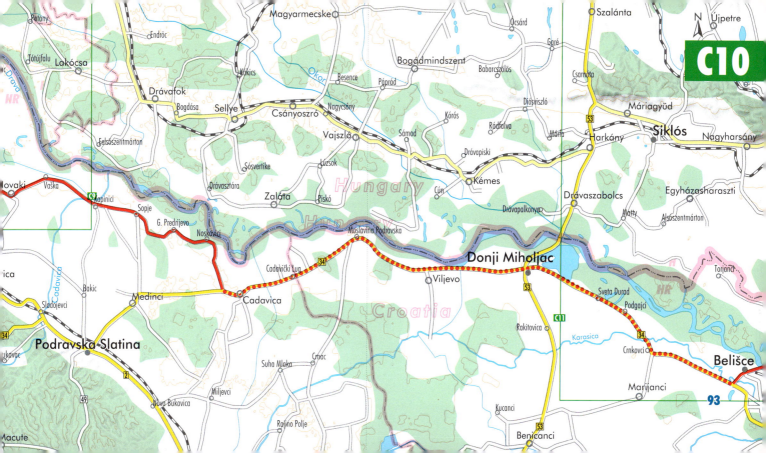

The through street passes by here. The current baroque building however has nothing in common with the church mentioned in the 11th century. The two castles at the edge of the park are also not built on old foundations. After the expulsion of the Turks, a noble family received the surrounding estates as a gift and built an 80 metre long, single story building in 1818 which follows the road. It has two ballrooms and 14 rooms. Nearly 100 years later, the significantly larger castle was built in the very popular Neo-Tudor style. They were connected with a covered hall. It now houses the city administration and is surrounded by a park.

The company Limex, which is known throughout Europe for its metal ware, has a prospering production facility. Also the location at the crossing of two highways with bridges over the Drau as well as the fundamentals for tourism provide hopes to the city. Once they got attention with the Miholjacko Sijelo (Miholjac Gathering) which is the most important event of the year with folk costumes, music and dance and an abundance of culinary offers.

### From Donji Miholjac (Croatia) to Bezdan (Serbia)          85 km

Continue in this direction. You will pass the large lakes which were established in the flood area of the Drau. Between the following villages of **Sveti Đurad** and **Podgajci Podravski**, you will find a narrow bayou which reaches to the road. About 100 metres further south, an old wooden bridge leads over the water and is a little romantic. Continue past the town of Kitišanci via **Črnkovci** and **Veliscovci**. Turn left after a further kilometre on the 34.

You will reach Belišće on the 517.

### Belišće

The city developed in 1884 as a settlement for workers of a large sawmill. The process of replacing huge Slavonian forest areas with fields was continued after World War II. Today it is still the home of one of the largest cellulose and paper industries although the market is stagnating. The city with a population of 12,000

offers numerous shopping and dining possibilities but has little to offer in terms of points of interest. The recently restored castle of the Gutmann family stands out in the surroundings, a neo-classical construction in gleaming white.

Continue further on the 517 which leads you around the industrial area and over the Drava. It follows the bayou in a large left curve and accompanies it for quite some time afterwards.

A memorial on the right with candles and flowers commemorates the war victims of 1992. The forest areas are mainly fenced in and signs warn you not to enter since the ground is contaminated with mines.

Continue a further five kilometres over lonely fields until you reach Baranjsko Petrovo Selo.

### Baranjsko Petrovo Selo

The town has a border crossing, which is only of regional meaning, is however more known for the Patarake Buše, the three day carnival. Those who

choose the nice "buša" (mask), dress in the traditional costume of the opposite gender. Men are also allowed to commit some mischief in the ugly, horned and very heavy wooden masks. On the last day, the evil spirit of the past year is burnt. This can for example take the form of "cold chicken" as a symbol of the bird flu. The road continues in numerous zigzags to Beli Manastir via Petlovac.

## Beli Manastir

Since 1920, the city with a population of 8.700 no longer belongs to Hungary. According to legend, the monastery in the village of Pel, Pel Monostor, became Beli Manastir, the white monastery. The population has always been multi ethnic: In 1910, 61 percent were German – and today the non-Serbian people who were expelled during the Croatian-Serbian war in the 1990's have returned, contributing to the mixture of ethnicities. The main ethnic groups are Croats, Serbs and Hungarians; Germans hardly play a role anymore. Trains travel directly to Pecs and Osijek from the train station.

You can continue around the centre to the north or to the south on the 517. In the east you will meet a crossroad, the 7/E 73, and continue to the north. Accompanied by lively traffic, you will soon pass through **Branjin Vrf** and after a further five kilometres you will reach the turn to Popovac by the town of Kneževo on the left.

**Tip:** When turning, take a look to the left. In 100 metres distance, where the road merges, you will find a park with an orthodox church, which appears rather oriental.

From **Popovac** continue to the left towards Branjina.

## Branjina

Here you can study the differences between the Christian and the Orthodox churches of the villages. However they are rarely as oriental as in the town of Kneževo.

The road follows the ridge to **Podolje** and **Draž** in large curves and is accompanied by a controlled river on the left. Draž is also the administrative seat for the community of Batina, which lies a further six kilometres and is half the size.

## Batina

At the beginning of town, the concrete bridge reaches over to Serbia. You should make the detour to visit the nice little town. On the left, wine cellars line the road which have been carved out of the steep cliff and appear as old cabins. The baroque church, which overlooks the town, would not be noticed much at a different location, but looks spectacular in this place. The town becomes narrower to the north and is shadowed by steep cliffs. On top of the cliffs there is an almost 30 metres tall monument and a permanent exhibition to commemorate the battle of Batina in 1944, in which the Soviet and Yugoslavian unions freed the area from the German troops.

A beautiful view over the Danube and it's numerous bayous is the reward for the climb. The small harbour town is still influenced by the agriculture, however now also offers tourists a temporary and a group of artists a permanent stay.

Border controls are performed before and after the bridge. The street bridges a bayou of the Danube on the Serb side and then turns to the north.

## The history of Serbia

Serbia was first mentioned in 822 and was under the rule of Byzantine for over one hundred years after the turn of the first century. In 1389, the Serb army was defeated by the Ottomans in the Battle of Amselfeld which was the end of the medieval Serbian State. From 1459 to 1804 it was a part of the Ottoman Empire. Although they initially paid tribute to the Ottomans, the Serbs were gradually able to acquire independence, which was officially recognised at the Congress of Berlin in 1878. A few years later, the princedom officially became a kingdom.

After the Austro-Hungarian successor to the throne, Franz Ferdinand, was killed by a Serb secret organization "Black Hand" in an attack in Sarajevo in 1914, a chain reaction brought about the outbreak of World War I. Thereby Serbia was on the side of the Entente Cordiale and hoped that the dissolution of Austria-Hungary would bring about a merger of the south Slavic people.

After the collapse of the dual monarchy, this actually became possible after the end of World War I. Serbia and Montenegro merged together to the new Kingdom of Serbs, Croats and Slovenes. The different religions of the people as well as their striving towards dominance in the new state was a problem from the beginning.

In order to overcome the inner-political problems resulting therefrom, King Alexander I created a military dictatorship with the goal of unifying the southern Slavic people. Despite armed resistance, a Serb dominated military and police state developed, which was in conflict with nearly all neighbours.

Upon the outbreak of World War II, the Kingdom of Yugoslavia initially remained neutral. Blinded by the success of the Germans and the "new formation" of southeast Europe, it joined the war in 1941 on the side of the German Empire. A military coup overthrew the regime a short time later and a friendship and mutual assistance pact was made with the Soviet Union. As a result, German and Italian troops marched into Yugoslavia and the country surrendered. Resistance was organised from abroad. Before the Red Army was able to take over control, the Communist Partisan Army of Josip Broz Tito controlled the country.

In 1945, the Federal People's Republic of Yugoslavia was declared which was closely bound to Moscow with a Friendship Pact. The economy has a socialist organisation, the political office of the Communist Party designed as a centre of power. In 1948 there was a separation from the UdSSR and the country attempted to take an independent turn towards socialism. The workers' self management was introduced and contracts were made with the west. In 1955, an official reconciliation between the Soviet Union and Yugoslavia was announced although the difference continued to occur. Not only because Yugoslavia played an active role within the movements of the block-free states.

Tito continued to expand his power and was elected president for life in 1963. Although Yugoslavia condemned the Prague Spring, the government internally continued to apply massive pressure on those who thought differently. Steps were taken towards federalisation.

These were not able to prevent the increase of tension after the death of Tito in 1980. Demands for more independence and economic development became louder, and protests broke out. Croats and Slovenes finally declared their independence. As a result, there were violent battles between the Serb-dominated Federal Armed Forces and the respective people's militia. The troops soon retreated from Slovenia, however a civil war then broke out in Croatia. The Federal Army thereby openly supported the Serbs. Mediation attempts by the European Union were without success, the country turned into a bloody chaos.

The result of the civil war was a final separation of the multiethnic Balkan States. Merely Serbia and Montenegro remained unified in the new "Federal Republic of Yugoslavia", however suffered from UN sanctions. At the end of 1995, the Serb President Slobodan Milošević signed a peace treaty in Dayton together with the presidents of Bosnia-Herzegovina and Croatia. A short time later Yugoslavia was officially recognised and the sanctions were abolished.

The situation escalated once again in 1998 when Serbia attempted to violently prevent independence for the Kosovo Albanians. NATO engaged in aerial warfare against Yugoslavia, which did not end until all armed Serb forces retreated from Kosovo in June 1999.

During the parliamentary and presidential elections in September 2000, massive accusa-

**Before the border crossing to Serbia**

tions of election fraud were made and a strike and protest movements brought the country to a standstill. Milošević was finally forced to recognize that the new president, Vojislav Koštunica, had won the election. In 2001, Milošević was turned over to the UN International Criminal Tribunal in The Hague where he died on March 11, 2006 of heart failure.

All of Serbia's attempts to keep the remaining area of Yugoslavia were unsuccessful. In 2006 Montenegro declared independence and two years later Kosovo also declared independence. It is however not recognised by many states.

Since 2006 the name of the Serbian state is the "Republic of Serbia".

Turn right after about 500 metres and continue through the fields towards Bezdan whereby you will cross two further bayous and a channel. The road eventually turns into a dusty gravel road.

## Bezdan

The town with a population of 5,200 does not have the character of a city, but it has shopping and dining possibilities. It is influenced by industrial art and agriculture and has some industry with a textile factory and a shipyard. The natural resources are in the forests, rivers and lakes. There are also thermal springs which allowed the construction of a modern health spa and rehabilitation centre in the 1990's.

After the expulsion of the Turks and the introduction of the Habsburg regime, Poles, Czechs and Germans settled here. The area is still multiethnic today although the mixture has changed. The last change came about from the immigration of Serbian refugees in the 1990's with the simultaneous emigration of

*Hungarians. These still form the majority with nearly 57 percent.*

## From Bezdan (Serbia)
## to Kelebia (Hungary)                    150 km

The R 662 leads you through the town and on to **Kolut** and further to Bački Breg.

### Bački Breg

*Germans and Hungarians settled in both towns in the 18th century, but the Serbs now dominate in Kolut and the Šokci in Bački Breg. The Šokci are an ethnic group, which mostly call themselves Croats. They maintain their own dialect, traditional costumes and customs, for example the carnival as already described by Baranjsko Petrovo Selo shortly before Beli Manastir. Before you cross the border, you can refresh yourself in the Balkan Guesthouse or purchase some drinks in one of the shops since the service can be more cumbersome than you are accustomed to.*

Continue to the north over **Hercegszántó**, **Dávod** and **Csátalja** on the 51. Then make a

"Welcome to Serbia!"

right, pass through the town and over the fields to the village Gara.

### Gara

*Apparently, the original location was on a hill four kilometres away. This may be where the name is from since it might be derived from a Slavic word for hill. It is however sure that the settlement was destroyed by the Turks and later rebuilt whereby the Germans also played a role.*

Turn right into the town and turn left again before the church. Continue straight ahead for the next eleven kilometres. The fields reach as far as the horizon and there is no shade to be found. You will reach **Bácsborsód** and di-

rectly afterwards **Bácsbokod**. After the church square, which has two memorials, turn right and you will soon find yourself between the rape seed fields again. One kilometre after the constructions, there is a fork in the road where you keep to the right. After eleven kilometres you will reach Bácsalmás.

### Bácsalmás

*The city is designed with regular right angles, which gives the impression that it was meticulously planned. This is, however, completely incorrect: Since the Turks conquered the area, the residing population disappeared so that Bunjevci (Bunjewatzen) could take its place. This Croatian group, which speaks its own dialect, settled in the entire region of Bácska, which belonged to Hungary until 1918. Large areas however then were lost to Serbia. The cultural centre of the catholic Bunjevci is 25 kilometres away behind the city of Subotica on the other side of the Serbian border. In the 1780's, after the country had come under Habsburg control, nearly three times as many Germans settled here, the so-called Donauschwaben. They* called their new home Heimerskirchen. In 1941, when the town had reached its highest population of 13,000, they still had a two-thirds majority.

After the expulsion and replacement with Hungarians from Slovakia, there are now 230 residents who belong to the German minority. The Croats are mostly assimilated so that only 125 people consider themselves Croatian. The population which had decreased, rose to over 8,000 in 1986. After the closing of several companies and the debtladen privatisation of the cooperations, the population of the rural town decreased again. A large number of unemployed remains without perspectives.

The Csauscher House with the cupola roof and classical decorations can be found behind the church. There is a memorial of the expulsion in the nearby park.

On the way to Csikéria you will cross the abandoned railroad tracks, which once travelled to Subotica and made Bácsalmás an important junction. In **Csikéria** the tradition of the Bunjevco has been maintained. Continue through the town after a left curve, pass the neo-gothic church and make a right at the end of town in the north. Once again you will find yourself between the fields.

You will be greeted by a shady forest, where you will find a little pink church on the right of the street which is designed and decorated like a large cathedral.

The neo-gothic church of St. Anna with the attractive windows belongs to the Baronmeierhof (Bárómajor) Redl, which stands in front of part of the castle building. This gothic building with an English influence currently serves as a shelter for the poor and also as a retirement home.

These are the main points of interest of Tompa, which you will reach on the heavily travelled 53 to the left.

## Tompa

The town with a population of 5,000 was granted city rights in 2004. During the Yugoslavian War, the 53 was detoured around the residential areas because the traffic had increased significantly, especially of the trucks. The town is a transit station for Adriatic Sea tourists and a shopping attraction for Serb border crossers, which has been reduced by the position of the outer border of the EU. Although 70 GmbHs (LTDs) have settled here, the agriculture of bell peppers, tomatoes and livestock has remained the same.

From Bárómajor you can cross straight over the 53 and continue through the forest to Kelebia in about four kilometres. If you would like to look around Tompa or spend the night, there are many possibilities, you can continue to the neighbouring town to the east.

## Kelebia

The city is a curiosity, as is often seen as a result of the Iron Curtain. The town was divided by the border and today exists twice. The separation in this case took place during World War I when most of the Vojvodina fell to Serbia. The Serb village of Kelebija, which developed from the north-western suburb of Subotica in the 1930's into a closed community, is now connected to Tompa at the border crossing. The north-eastern Hungarian Kelebia, which has become wider since the crossing of the Danube, is now larger than the twin sister but appears to have less possibilities of developing. The train station and the abundance of forests and water might turn it into a recreational area for Subotica. Trains travel directly from here to Budapest and Belgrade.

## Escape of Jörg Berger

The junior selection of the GDR played against Yugoslavia in Subotica, near the Hungarian border, in March 1979. In the night before the game, the national coach of the GDR, Jörg Berger, left the hotel unnoticed and took a train to Belgrade at 5:00 a. m.. In the embassy of the Federal Republic of Germany he received a fake passport with the name Gerd Prenzel and travelled with the "Orient Express" from Belgrade to Frankfurt am Main.

His disappearance was already reported in the Yugoslavian media. During the control between Yugoslavia and Austria, he told the border guard that his passport was stolen which was why the embassy issued a new one for his return travel. Jörg Berger described the decisive situation in his book: "Meine zwei Halbzeiten Ein Leben in Ost und West" as such: The customs officer "gave me my (faked as Gerd Prenzel) passport back, looked me deep in the eyes, smiled and said: "And now, Mr. Berger, good luck in the west!"

There he was able to continue his career as a football coach of many Bundesliga teams. He was especially know as the "rescuer" and prevented Eintracht Frankfurt from being relegated on two occasions. In the west he was also observed by the Stasi and in the GDR he was considered a "traitor". He did not accept a position as coach for the West Berlin football club Hertha BSC because the risk for him was much higher there than in West Germany.

As Jörg Berger stated in an interview in 2009: "I had the same nightmares for at least two years: I was in the GDR again, was kidnapped or travelled there with the sport and was not able to return. Every time I woke up covered in sweat. It was so intensive that at the first moment I didn't know: Is it true?"

Cross the railroad tracks in Kelebia and continue in the same direction towards the 55. After passing several points, make a slight right turn. Continue in large zigzags through forest areas and fields until you reach Ásotthalom. Follow the 55 for seven kilometres until you reach Mórahalom. If you would like to avoid the highly travelled road, turn right on the **Köztársaság utca** after entering **Ásotthalom** and continue in zigzag to the next town, which is nearly twice as long.

Leave the main road in **Mórahalom** and continue towards the south which is a more comfortable journey. Continue towards **Röszke** and past scattered farmsteads. After you have crossed the autobahn M 5/E 75 and the railroad tracks to Horgoš and Subotica, you will reach the border town on a branch of the Theiß. The little road to the left leads to Szeged via **Szentmihálytelek**.

### Szeged

The city lies in a sharp curve of the Theiß (szeg = corner) and was founded by the Romans under the name Partiscum, which appears to have later become a base of Attila the Hun. After the immigration of the Hungarians in the 10th century, it gradually became the centre of the salt trade. The Turks pillaged the town in 1526 and occupied it for 143 years. With the recapture, a phase of growth began, which was however slowed down by the witch trials.

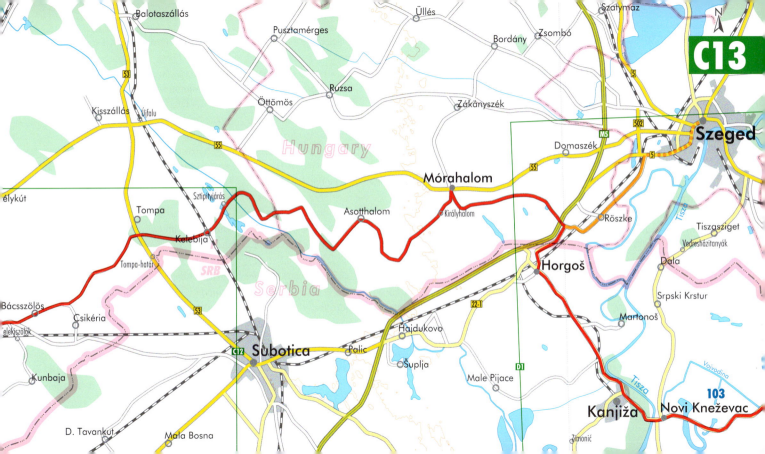

In 1879, 95 percent of the town were destroyed by catastrophic flooding. The locals were able to make the best out of this misfortune: With international help, a completely new city was planned which not only lead to the radial structure with the circular roads but also to a balanced appearance with the mixture of historical and Jugendstil. However, the upswing was slowed in 1918 by the loss of the southern areas to Romania and Serbia. A sustained positive development did not begin again until after World War II. The food production was expanded to an industry, substantial crude oil findings brought jobs and numerous educational institutions were developed.

The abundance of points of interest make a longer stay necessary. Here we will only take a small walk through the centre. The massive Votive Church in neo-Romanesque style is prominent an very impressive. The construction began prior to World War I and was completed in 1930 as the fourth largest church in Hungary. To the left in front of the tower facade, you will find the octagonal Demetrius Tower, which was revealed during construction and dates back to the 13th century making it the oldest building of the city. On the Dome Square, which corresponds in size to the Marcus Square in Venice, open air events take place in the summer including operas, drama and folklore. This square is especially suitable for this purpose since it is surrounded by the National Memorial Hall on three sides. In the arcades, famous people are commemorated with statues. The musical clock in the middle of the facade plays at 12:15 and 16:15 for nine minutes and shows revolving figures.

To the right behind the dome you will find a baroque tower of the Serbian Orthodox Church. It has an iconostasis in rococo style, carved in pear wood with 80 icons. To the right of the building with the clock, you can exit the square through an arcade. If you turn right at the second possibility through the Jókai utca, you reach the almost triangular Dugonics tér. On the right you will find the administrative building of the university and behind that, on the corner of Kárász utca, you will find the Unger-Mayer House which has an elaborate Jugendstil roof from 1911. It is hard to see from this square since it is the end of a long shopping mile and is often very busy, which is also increased by the mobile traders.

After the next corner, you will find the Reök Palace in a significantly smaller triangular square. The palace also has an impressive jugendstil facade whereby the roof has remained simple.

Continue on the circular road Tisza Lajos körút to the second road on the left, the Gutenberg utca. This road leads to the large New Synagogue which was built in 1907 in a combination of common styles. The exterior is no longer attractive, but the interior radiates festiveness with a variety of forms and colours. Continue straight ahead on the Hajnóczy utca on the other side of the building until you reach Klauzál tér where you can take a break in the most well-known café in the city, Virág-kávéház. The site was ennobled since the revolutionary Lajos Kossuth held his last speech in 1849 from the balcony of the big white building, the Kárász house, before he fled into exile. Trains travel from Szeged directly to Budapest and Subotica.

# From Szeged/Horgos to the Iron Gate near Kladovo

**477 km**

At the train station in Szeged

### From Szeged/Horgos to Kikinda          75 km

If you are travelling with the train from Hungary, you can travel comfortably from Budapest to Szeged. The regional train from here to Horgos in Serbia consists of two silver-coloured diesel locomotives of a different generation. The ride is rather bumpy. The Hungarian border guard controls directly at the border in a small train station, the Serbian control is performed at the train station in Horgos.

From the train station in Horgos, continue on the **Zeleznicka** into the small centre of the town.

**Tip:** The blue-white road signs provide information in three languages: in Cyrillic and Latin script and also in Hungarian, in this case "Vasút Utca".

At the roundabout in the centre of Horgos you will find numerous stores. You will also find exchange possibilities and overnight accommodation, such as the City Café on the right side. In case you arrive on a Sunday and the banks are closed, you can exchange Euro into Serbian Dinar in a small store on the right side towards the end of town. There are direct connections from the train station to Subotica and Szeged.

Follow the road from Horgos to Kanjiza. Continue 13 kilometres on the well paved road past corn and sunflower fields, which are typical for the Vojvodina region. Keep to the left towards Kanjiza and Novi Knezevac shortly before entering the town. The sign with the name of the town is also in three different

Pub in Kanjiza

languages whereby the Hungarian name of Magyarkanizsa indicates the large ethnic portion of Hungarians (48 % in the autonomous region of Vojvodina.

At the beginning of town a transformer tower serves as an advertising medium: "Room available – Family – Sobe". Behind the Old Tisa Pub, which is painted red, you will reach a square. To the left leads towards Novi Knezevac. On the right side at the end of town you will find a large recreational and hotel complex.

You will cross the Theiß on the quiet, smooth paved road and continue slightly downhill to **Novi Knezevac**. From here follow the signs to Banatsko Aranđelovo first to the right, then to the left. The road first leads you a good distance around Novi Knezevac and can be irritating. Continue to the right at a fork in the road on a well paved road, past lakes and lonely farmsteads.

In the centre of **Banatsko Aranđelovo** (Hungarian Oroszlámos), turn right towards Podlokanj and Kikinda. At the football field of FK Slavia, a store, which is painted green, invites you to take a break. It is easy to enter into a conversation with the locals.

The town is rather long, but after the sign at the end of town you will again find endless sunflower and corn fields. The road becomes lonely after **Podlokanj** and concrete slabs replace the pavement. Some of them are rather deteriorated, but even worse are the many tiny flies from the corn and sunflower fields.

*In Crna Bara*

Continue past the small town of **Vrbica**, which is called Egyházaskér in Hungarian, and further on concrete slabs until you reach Crna Bara (Hungarian Feketetó). The picture is similar: lonely houses on the side of the road, wooden electrical and phone poles and endless fields again once you have exited the town.

## Crna Bara

*Crna Bara is somewhat larger and has numerous interesting churches and a few small stores. The small grocery stores are usually colourfully painted and you will often find refrigerators in front of them with beverages. Tourist might often wonder how it is possible for three or four stores to survive in such a small area – but it seems to work.*

After a further eleven kilometres you will reach the town of Mokrin which also has churches worth visiting.

## Mokrin

*The supply situation is excellent, as is common for Serbia. Well stocked stores offer beverages and daily articles. With a few words of Serbian, the residents are open and friendly and you will soon notice that tourists are normally quite welcome in Serbia. As a cyclist you will usually also receive extra sympathy.*

It is a further 14 kilometres from Mokrin to Kikinda. The surface of the road is in good condition here. Despite the low amount of traffic, you should be careful since the young Serbs occasionally drive too fast on such smooth and lonely roads.

## Kikinda

*The city of Kikinda has a population of 42,000 and in the district of Severni Banat*

*In Kikinda*

in the Serbian provice of Vojvodina. It's name was first mentioned in the 15th century as Kökenud, which described – together with the term Ezehida – this small region with many small villages.

*Kikinda has numerous churches worth visiting, the very popular national theatre which is open year round, a lively pedestrian area, many stores and various cafés. Trains travel directly from the station to the Romanian Jimbola.*

*There are not very many places, which offer overnight accommodation. The simplest* and most comfortable can be found in the Hotel Narvik. Officially it is a four star hotel, however the charm of the 1970's gives the impression of two or three stars less. You can easily story your bicycle in the underground garage. This hotel is very expensive for Serbian conditions. A double room with breakfast costs 4,800 Serbian Dinar. (The exchange rate in January 2010 was 1:97 to the Euro) The bakery next to the hotel is, however, very inexpensive. A pizza costs about 40 Dinar in a café, a cappuccino about 55 Dinar.

## From Kikinda to Begejci/Žitište     67 km

From the centre, follow the Hauptstraße towards Nakovo (border crossing to Romania) and then turn towards Srpska Crnja and Rusko Selo. On the left side after exiting town, someone attempted to construct a small private castle. Now the grass is growing on the large piece of property and the incomplete building appears sad. The

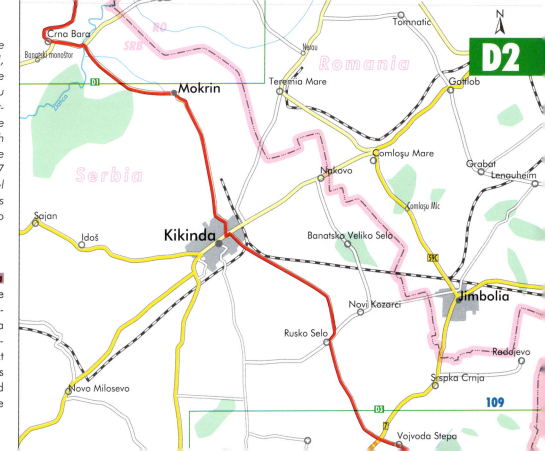

Sign in Begejci

then turn left towards Srpska Crnja and Nova Crnja. On the main road that leads to Srpska Crnja on the left and Nova Crnja on the right, continue straight ahead and you will soon reach **Vojvoda Stepa** where the little store "Bife Grand" welcomes tourists. Continue straight ahead on the newly constructed road to Srpski Itebej. It is nearly 17 kilometres from Vojvoda Stepa to Srpski Itebej. Occasionally you will see rows and groups of trees. You will find yourself in the middle of the fields. It is important to drink plenty while in extreme temperatures and bright sunshine!

Continue through the town of **Srpski Itebej** and follow the road to **Begejci**. The road makes a right curve after the town and a road to the left leads to Meda. Turn left at a crossing six kilometres after Srpski Itebej. Currently there are no street signs. If you continue straight ahead you will reach Ban Karadordevo. Follow the road to the left towards Begejci.

After about four kilometres the road makes a 90 degree turn to the left. After the curve you

will find an illegal waste dump on the side of the road. After two further kilometres you will reach **Begejci**.

A blue and white sign on the side of the road shows: to the right you will reach Novi Sad, Zrenjanin, Zitiste and Beograd. To the left you will reach Secanj.

**Tip:** The Iron Curtain Trail leads to the left towards Secanj, however since overnight accommodation is scarce in this area, you should first continue to the right to the neighbouring town of Zitiste.

It is nearly six kilometres from Begejci to Žitište. Shortly before you reach the town, follow the signs to the right towards Zitiste. On this street sign the towns are only written in Cyrillic. Afterwards continue through the town of Zitiste until you reach the 7. Opposite the crossing you will find the Motel Kozara.

### Žitište

*In the motel you can get a room and breakfast for 1,000 Serbian Dinar. Since the 7 leads to the Romanian border crossing by Jimbolia, many*

paved road is hardly travelled so you will not be disturbed on your journey through the flat landscape. Turn right in **Rusko Selo** towards Nova Crnja. Continue a short distance and people use this overnight accommodation and the large restaurant is also very busy in the evening hours. When the weather is nice you can sit outside on the small terrace. You should absolutely try the mixed meat platter for dinner. The selection and amount of grilled treats is great. You should also try a Schopska salad with tomatoes, cucumbers and Bulgarian feta cheese. The Jelen Pivo is a great beer which can be recommended. For breakfast they serve the usual ham with egg and toast.

### From Begejci/Žitište to Vršac                95 km

From Žitište follow the same route back to Begejci. There you can replenish your supplies.

Follow the road to Krajisnik, Sutjeska and Secanj. Shortly after the town sign of **Krajisnik** turn right towards **Sutjeska**. There you can enjoy a coffee or soft drink in a small café across from the sports field of FK Radinchki. Continue your journey on the Hauptstraße until you reach the 7-1 where you turn left towards Vršac. It is about 65 kilometres to Vršac.

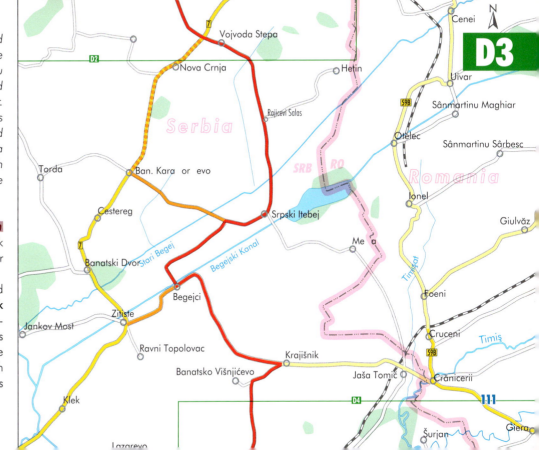

Vršac

## Secanj

*In the next town of Secanj you will find overnight accommodation and you can decide if you would like to take a break or continue to Vršac. Everywhere you will find little stores, kiosks and stands on the side of the road. Therefore you will never have difficulties finding beverages or necessities on the Serbian section.*

Continue on the 7-1 which makes a right in Secanj at a crossing with a large Lukoil petrol station. The road to Vršac is smooth and is excellent for making headway. Be careful, occasionally you will see a truck on this road!

**Boka, Konak, Hajdučica, Velika Greda,** Plandište and Margita are all very similar: The houses with their small gardens run along the street in a row. A church provides a change of scenery and kiosks and little stores provide a good fundamental supply. The landscape in this region however appears somewhat monotonous and you will be happy to make good headway in this section. The smooth pavement and the level landscape offer the best possibilities for this purpose.

**Plandište** appears very well kept and inviting. Continue to follow the 7-1 to the left and you will reach a supermarket on the right. After the town you will be able to see the mountains Vršacki Breg by Vršac. The highest is Guduricka Vrh with an elevation of 639 metres.

In **Margita** the Kafana/Bar Disneyland lies on the right. There you can rest on the terrace and enjoy a beverage or a small

Vineyard by Vršac

snack before you take on the remaining 15 kilometres of the stretch. The last section to Vršac is beautiful. You will be happy with the mountains already in sight and the smooth level street. Shortly after Margita you will cross the small river Moravica. Honey is frequently offered on the side of the road which is directly from the adjacent sunflower fields. You can see the beehives and some of the beekeepers live here in their trailers.

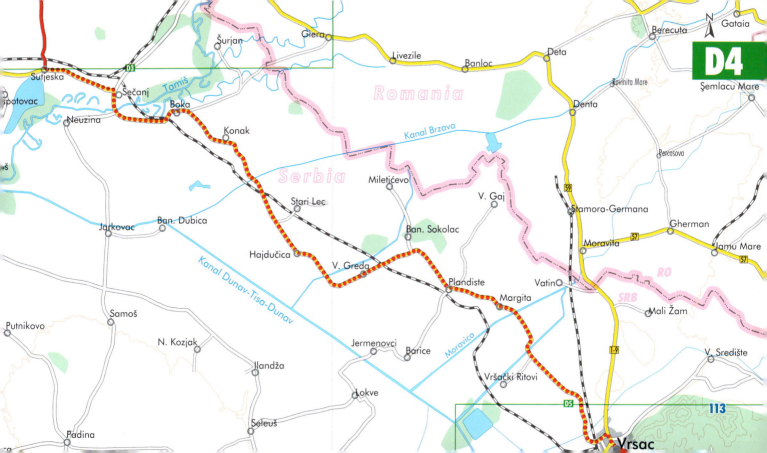

## Vršac

In the attractive city centre of Vršac you will almost automatically come to the large three star hotel "Srbija". A double room here costs about Euro 45. This is a lot for Serbian standrads but you have a good view of the city from the hotel room and it is only a few metres to the pedestrianised zone. The bicycles can be safely stored in the basement. The small city with a population of about 37,000 lies in the Serbian district of Južni Banat. Belgrade is about 100 kilometres from here. The Romanian border is about ten kilometres from here. Nearly 6,000 residents are of Romanian origin and also numerous Romanians and Hungarians live in Vršac. The town is known for the surrounding vineyards and the basketball team Hemopharm Vršac, which played in the Millennium Sport Centre that was built in 2002 and became well known throughout Europe.

The city centre surprisingly has renovated old buildings and there are any shopping and dining possibilities. You should enjoy a cup of coffee in the Grand Hotel on the main square of the city centre. You will find many possibilities for exchanging currencies. Trains travel directly from the station to Belgrade, Timisoara, Bucharest and Belgrade.

### From Vršac to Bela Crkva　　　　45 km

From the **Zarka Zrenjanin** turn into the **Dimitrija Tucovića**, which leads towards Mesic, Kuštilj and Vršacko Brdo. After you have left the town, continue slightly uphill past the vineyards. To the left is Guduricka Vrh with an elevation of 639 metres. On the right you will soon see the vineyard Vršacki Vinogrado. The road is smooth and little travelled. The surrounding landscape is beautiful.

Keep to the right at the fork in the road towards Kuštilj and at the next fork as well. Continue over a rather hilly area through large sunflower fields. At times you will have to conquer a 10 % uphill grade. Turn right again at the third fork in the road, however this time not towards

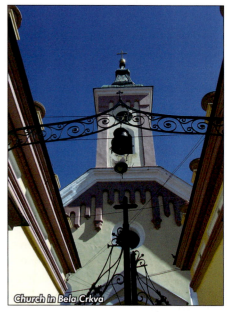

Church in Bela Crkva

Kuštilj but rather towards **Vojvodinci**. This is a very sleepy village. Turn right in town and shortly afterwards downhill with a 10 % grade.

**Dobrievo** is just as sleepy as the previous village. There are hardly any direct connections which can be travelled to Bela Crkva although several maps on the internet claim the opposite. Local residents assured us that one must travel via Jasenovo. Therefore, continue on the main road in Dobrievo, which leads towards Banatska Subotica.

## Banatska Subotica

*Here you will find a very attractive, restored church. There is also a small village store. A red star over the door remains from the time of the Yugoslavian Federation.*

After Banatska Subotica you will reach the 7-1 which leads to the target of the day, Bela Crkva. Shortly after crossing the railroad tracks, you will reach the town of **Jasenovo** which greets the cyclist with poor road conditions. Continue on the 7-1 to the left towards Bela Crkva. On the corner you will find a guest house with guest rooms but you should continue your journey to the interesting Bela Crkva, which you will reach after a further 13 kilometres.

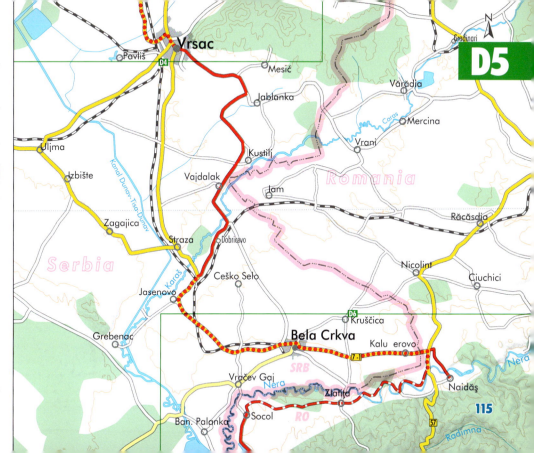

The road is smooth again after Jasenovo. You will once again cross the old railroad tracks which are hardly used, if it all, and continue through **Crvena Crkva** until you reach Bela Crkva after a short distance.

## Bela Crkva

This small town near the Romanian border has a population of about 12,500 and lies in the district of Vojvodina, in the Serbian part of Banat, on the foothills of the Carpathian mountains. Many Germans once lived here, but left the region after World War II. Apart from Serbs, many Romanians, Czechs, Romanians and Hungarians live here today.

In the Uliza Partizanska 66 you will find a very nice private guest house directly next to the restaurant on the corner. You can spend the night here for around ten Euros per person. There are good sanitary facilities and the rooms are very quiet.

Quite a few old constructions have been maintained in the city centre. The low stone and wooden houses and the trees along the roads remind of Irkutsk in Siberia. There are

*At the Nera*

many inviting historical churches, stores and cafés. A telecommunication business also offers the possibility of internet access.

### From Bela Crkva to Berzasca by the Danube  95 km

Follow to **Uliza Partizanska** towards Kalđuerovo and the border crossing to Romania. The next eleven kilometres pass by extensive vineyards. The pavement is good and there is hardly any traffic. After a long ascend with a twelve percent grade, the pavement

becomes better and you continue downhill through **Kalđuerovo**. Soon the Serb border crossing will be in sight.

## The history of Romania

Today's Romania is mostly on the territory of the former Danube Principalities of Moldavia and Wallachia as well as Transylvania. From the first century, the areas had been an integrated part of the Roman Empire. The population is therefore mostly romanised. During the migration however, ethnic groups came from the east which replaced a large number of the residents.

In the 13th century, the Romanians were officially mentioned for the first time and the first states were formed in Wallachia and Moldavia. They were able to become independent from Hungary, but soon afterwards extensive tributary payments had to be made to the Ottoman Empire in order to maintain their newly acquired independence.

Attempts to unify all Romanians in one empire were unsuccessful. Russia had a

great influence on the region until the Crimean Wars in 1853/54. During the 18th century, a Romanian national consciousness developed, which peaked in the merging of Moldavia and Wallachia under the name "Romania" in 1862. The country's sovereignty was recognised as sovereign in 1878 at the Berlin Congress.

Romania was initially neutral in World War I, but declared war against Austria-Hungary in the August of 1916. Resulting territorial losses remained temporary and were sometimes even turned into gains of additional land due to agreements in later peace treatis.

In the period between the wars, a great dissatisfaction developed with the established political parties and especially right-wing parties gained power. The inner-political crisis finally became an open dictatorship in 1938. After the outbreak of World War II, Romania was initially neutral however supported the Axis powers after the defeat of France.

After the forced resignation of Karl II, a pro-fascist military dictatorship came to power.

Zlatita - beginning of town

Romania became a member of the Tripartite Pact and supported the German Empire in their fight against the Soviet Union. After the defeat of the German Empire, the regime collapsed in 1944. As a result, there was an unconditional surrender and the Soviet armed forces occupied the country.

After the war, communist forces gained power, an agricultural reform resulted in the loss of large amounts of property and the collectivisation came into effect. Non-communist parties were prohibited and in 1947 the People's Republic of Romania was declared.

Afterwards the country was quickly integrated into the Soviet jurisdiction, and became part of the Cominform Pact and the Warsaw Pact (1955). After the retreat of the Soviet occupation troops in 1958, Romania was able to take a more independent route. The Secretary General Nicolae Ceauşescu established an increasingly totalitarian system influenced by an absurd personality cult with main support from the merciless secret police.

The country also had a critical course in respect of the Soviet Union: It did not take part in the occupation of Czechoslovakia in 1968 after the Prague Spring and distanced itself from the invasion of Afghanistan. The disastrous economic situation and the disrespect of human rights lead to a national uprising, spurred on by the general change in Europe. The dictator Ceauşescu was overthrown by the public and executed together with his wife Elena in December 1989.

The democratisation began thereafter: Parties reappeared which were prohibited before and free elections were performed. The situation however remained unstable. There were numerous turbulences and changes of government occurred over short periods of time. The integration to the west was however successful: In 2004, the country became a member of NATO and in 2007 it became a member of the EU.

The Romanian side of the border crossing appears quite run-down. Cars only pass here occasionally and the barriers are opened by hand. After the border crossing, continue on a stretch slightly uphill until you reach the road towards Orova and Zlatita where you turn right down the hill. It can occur that the dogs that made a riot upon your arrival, and were quiet during the border processing, follow you and bark aggressively.

Once you have reached the bottom, turn right at an abandoned observation site into a sandy road and continue towards Zlatita.

You will follow the course of the Nera on the sandy road. Follow the gravel road through the villages of **Lescovita**, **Kusić**, **Zlatita**, **Parneaura**, **Câmpia** and **Socol**. Town signs

At the Danube before Moldova Noua

will usually not be found. The buildings look completely different than on the Serbian side. In general, everything appears lonelier and poorer.

The landscape appears rougher and broken-up. The mountain sides, the valley and the interesting course of the Nera make up for the strain of the bumpy road. After a few kilometres, you will see a large ruins on the right where a bridge crosses the Nera. The road is partially paved afterwards but in **Zlatita** it is of fine sand. You will find an old rusty sign at the beginning of town which is great for orienta-

tion. Afterwards the landscape becomes flatter and more docile. The impressive mountainsides by Lescovita are now behind you.

Continue through the town of **Câmpia** on sand and concrete and you will get a good impression of the country lifestyle in Romania. After **Socol**, you will reach a smooth paved road which you follow to the left if you do not want to view the centre of town. From here on it is easier again and you will make faster progress. Soon you will see the Danube and you can look forward to a completely new section of the Iron Curtain Trail.

You will follow the course of the Danube for several kilometres along the border between Serbia and Romania. Continue on the Romanian side until you reach the first dam. There is a road along the shores on the Serbian side, however due to the many hills and tunnels it is more difficult and dangerous to travel. Soon you will notice a red and white stone on the side of the road which indicates the following towns: Bazias 3 km, Pojejena 21 km etc. A very helpful rock!

You will reach **Bazias** on this very quiet road where you will find a restaurant with a wooden facade and a large covered terrace directly next to the water. The next town is Divici with a very small chapel at the beginning of town.

## Divici

*Colourful houses line the streets here. There is no room for trees along the road and the electrical lines cross back and forth over the road. Shopping and dining possibilities are rather rare, which is why it is recommended to always have some provisions with you.*

Continue towards **Belobrasca** and **Pojejena**. It is 39 kilometres from here to Berzasca. Cross over the Pojejena and continue on the smooth street through a quite level landscape which is characterised by fields, meadows and rows of trees. Shortly before you reach Moldova Noua you will find a petrol station on the right where you can exchange money and do some shopping.

## Moldova Veche/Moldova Noua

*Continue on the main road past the centre of Moldova Veche. On the right you will see the*

Towards Berzasca

residential area of the city. The town lies south east of Moldova Noua in the region of Banat. It has a population of 12,000 and correspondingly good shopping possibilities.

The landscape remains flat after Moldova Veche. Continue on the paved road towards Coronini. On a hillside on the left you will see a large factory for the processing of copper which has seen better days.

You will find a more pleasing sight in Coronini.

## Coronini

*As in Divici, colourful houses dominate the appearance. The shopping possibilities are*

limited here. Coronini lies right next to the rocky shores of the Danube. The hillsides are closer to the Danube here than on the rest of the stretch.

This is where the beautiful section on the Danube route begins. The hills on both sides of the Danube become steeper and more rocky. The road winds along directly next to the shore and you can enjoy a wonderful view. The following kilometres are some of the best Europe's roads have to offer. It is a shame however that the road is made of gravel in many sections. The road conditions vary between good and bad. The beautiful landscape however makes up for the burden! Although the road is not highly travelled, you should be very careful in the curves.

**Tip:** Between Coronini and the turn to Sichevita, you will find the restaurant Sandvas on the left of the road. The fish dishes are very recommendable there. On an inviting terrace there is a small fountain and under the umbrella you can enjoy your meal and the Romanian Ursus beer. Food and drink costs about Euro 10 per person. The prices for tourists are significantly higher in Romania than in Serbia.

Here you will find a freshly paved section of road. The landscape is somewhat flatter, the valley of the Danube widens and is not quite as spectacular. The road continues somewhat distanced from the shores of the Danube past fields of corn. Continue through the town of **Liubcova** and after a few kilometres you will reach Berzasca.

## Berzasca

*Next to the shores of the Danube you will find the newly constructed guest house – "Pensiunea Isabella". For an equivalent of € 10 you can spend the night in a double room. If you are lucky, you will have a direct view of the river. In any case, you can enjoy the covered terrace. On the main road you will find the small café/bar "Luiza" which is run by a very nice elderly couple.*

## From Berzasca to Kladovo          100 km

Continue along the shores of the Danube towards Orova and Drobeta-Turnu Severin. Abandoned factories and rotten residential buildings disturb the landscape by Drenvoca. The cliffs along the Danube become steeper and soon you will be rewarded with a beautiful view. The course of the road on the Serbian side can be recognised by numerous bridges and curves. Numerous tunnels had to be made in the rocks. On the Romanian side the course of the road hardly has any tunnels. The road conditions however vary greatly. You will find sections of smooth pavement, then dusty gravel roads that are difficult to travel on and the occasional construction site.

Cross over the Glaucina and you will soon reach the town of **Svinita**. The road is somewhat better afterwards. You will pass a unique opening at the river Tişovia. It is a further 12 kilometres from here to Dubova.

Now and then you will see observation points of metal which are already showing their age. The section before Dubova is rather exhausting. The road moves away from the shores of the Danube and runs through the adjacent mountains.

## Dubova

*You will find two dining possibilities in Dubova and a small store in which you can purchase various beverages and snacks.*

Continue downhill after Dubova until you reach the shores of the Danube once again. The most attractive part of the Danube stretch begins here.

**Tip: Once again you will see impressive cliffs along the shore and the little white cloister Mraconia invites you to take a break.**

*A little further on the left you will find the highest rock sculpture in Europe with a height of 40 metres. It represents the Dacian King Decebalus. After ten years of work by twelve sculptors, the initiator I.C. Drgan created a memorial in 2004: "Decebalus Rex – Dragan Fecit" is the inscription.*

The road continues to wind until you reach the town on Eşelniţa.

## Eşelniţa

*The town stretches over four kilometres and a lot of it with the support of the European Union. Here you will find numerous dining possibili-*

ties and also overnight accommodation such as the guest houses "Steaua Dunarii" and "La Ponton". The for the region typical fish dishes can be recommended.

**Tip:** On the left side of the street lies the Mala Perla Dunarii where you can pitch your tent. There are various shopping possibilities in the town. Since the town of Orşova is not far away, the need for new provisions should not be all that big.

It is however an exhausting journey to conquer. The road leads away from the Danube and leads over the mountain with a downhill grade of 11 %.

### Orşova

The city lies in a curve of the Danube and is a very popular tourist destination. The numerous small and large boats in the harbour are proof thereof. You can spend the night in the three star hotel "Meridian" but there are also many other possibilities. There are also many shopping possibilities.

There is nothing left of the old city centre to view. Until 1973, the current was so strong at

*Observation house at the Danube*

the Iron Gate, the narrow point of the Danube, that the ships had to be towed upstream with a locomotive. Attempts to widen the river in the 19th century were not of any help. After the construction of the dam, the Danube became so wide and deep that it is now safe to travel with two watergates. Several villages and the island Ada Kaleh as well as the city centre of Orşova were victims of the rising water masses and had to be rebuilt at a higher level.

After passing the city, you will reach the E 70 which leads to Drobeta-Turnu Severin on the

right. Follow the road and cross the mouth of the river Cerna on a large bridge. A few metres further on the left you will find the train station of Orşova. The railroad tracks wind along the shores of the Danube towards Drobeta-Turnu Severin.

**Tip:** A little further ahead you will find a few tables and benches directly next to the shores of the Danube where you can take a rest. The view is beautiful. You look down on the wide Danube, over to the Serbian shores and on the city of Orşova. An especially interesting site is however no longer visible: the sunken island Ada Kaleh.

## Ada Kaleh

It was a Turkish enclave until 1912 and with its fortification, the palace, the Orthodox Church and the bazaar, it was a top level tourist destination and shopping paradise until the construction of the Romanian-Yugoslavian dam. The predominantly Turkish population was against relocating to a different island and most of them moved to Turkey.

At the Danube by Orşova

From now on you should be very careful since it cannot be avoided to travel on the highway for a short distance until you reach the first dam. The traffic is quite intensive and you especially need to watch out for the trucks. You should be prepared for the tunnel – Tunelul Bahna: Turn on your light, attach reflectors to your clothing and carefully keep as far to the right as possible. After the not too long tunnel it is not much further until you reach the border crossing which is before and after the dam. The route to

Serbia is simply signposted with "Belgrade 290 km".

*Between the control points you can cycle along the dam with the two hydro-power plants and two water-gates while you enjoy the view. The dam was built between 1964 and 972. The water level at this location was increased upstream by not less than 35 metres. Be careful when taking pictures! Keep in mind, you are in the border area!*

After the journey along the Romanian shores of the Danube, you now have several kilometres ahead of you in the Republic of Serbia. First continue to the left towards Niš and Kladovo. You will make good progress on the smooth pavement with little traffic through the towns of **Novo Sip** and **Kladusnica** until you reach Kladovo. The Romanian city Drobeta-Turnu Severin greets from the opposite shore of the Danube.

## Kladovo

*In Wallachian-Romanian this small harbour city is called Claudia. It is situated in the district*

At the Iron Gate

*of Bor and is the centre of the large community of the same name. A little over 9,000 people liver here. There are several dining and shopping possibilities. You can spend the night for a reasonable price in the hotel "Đerdap". The food is also very good here: Schopska salad, a selection of meats and potatoes provide a traditional and tasty evening meal. Served with a cold Jelen-Pivo.*

# From the Iron Gate near Kladovo to Kyustendil 446 km

From the hotel "Đerdap", continue on the Uferstraße without returning to the city centre. Shortly before you reach **Mala Vrbica** the land surface becomes narrower until you are cycling on a dam which separates a wide bayou of the Danube from the main stream.

*In the middle of the river lies the Romanian island Şimian which was intended to accommodate the population of Ada Kaleh, including the historical buildings, prior to them disappearing under the water. However, it was not possible to set up a working community without the good will of the "exotic" residents.*

The small – mala – Vrbica is followed by the large – velika – **Vrbica** where you can purchase some drinks in a small store. It is easy to start a conversation with the locals and they will certainly admire your bicycle.

The route to Negotin makes a small detour and follows the curve of the Danube. This guarantees quiet streets. The local residents will be very surprised to find a foreigner in this remote part of Serbia. Continue on the fairly

Storm on the Danube by Kladovo

good pavement over fields and meadows to **Korbovo** via **Rtkovo**. The strong winds can be exhausting over this open area. The pavement becomes smoother after Korbovo. From here it is about eight kilometres to **Vajuga**. Time appears to have come to a stop in this town with the many old buildings. You will reach the E 771 after **Milutinovac** which leads directly from Kladovo to Negotin. Turn left towards Velesnica, Grabovica and Negotin. You will have a slight hill to conquer before reaching Velesnica but you will be rewarded for the burden in Grabovica.

### Grabovica

*You should take a break at the restaurant "Stare Gajde" – Old Bagpipe. You can sit outside when the weather is nice.*

Continue along the shores of the Danube until you reach **Brza Palanka** which you will find after the sharp left curve of the river.

Between **Kupziste** and **Slatina** you can leave the road to the left to follow a narrow road directly next to the Danube. The location is however not easy to recognize. In the distance you will see a forest and a hill on which the road makes a right curve.

There is no road from there, where a sign points to the "Restoran Afrodita" where you should find the "Domace Kuhinie" – home kitchen. There are a few boats on the shore at the foot of a high observation tower. Continue over the bridge and then continue along the river. First the road is paved, then sandy, then grassy and overgrown. It is not possible to continue through here!

Follow the main road until you come to the Cyrillic sign to Mihajlovac. Turn left on a narrow, paved road through the fields

Vajuga

the Danube and the reeds along the shores. After about six or seven kilometres you will reach the small village of Kusjak where the road distances itself from the Danube.

## Kusjak

*Here you will find a nice restaurant on the right side of the street. In the café/bar "Laguna" you can enjoy a coffee or a beer inside or in the garden. The owner is very friendly and is happy to talk to you. Once you continue your journey, you can look down on the second dam from a hill.*

The road becomes smoother and wider and leads straight to Negotin.

into the town where you will also find a small store. Continue on the route and in the neighbouring town of **Novo Selo** you will come to a gravel road which is fairly good to travel that runs directly along the shores of the Danube. The stretch is very pretty. There are several parts with thick underbrush, in other places you have an open view of the water of

View of Đerdap 2

## Negotin

The Serbian city of Negotin lies in the district of Bor and has a population of about 18,000. It was mentioned for the first time in 1530. It is however assumed that the city, which became a modern centre for education and economy after the Serbian Revolution (1804-1833) in the 19th century, is much older. In the mean time, it lost it's leading position to Zaječar. The museum has numerous archaeological findings, some of which date back to Roman times. There are numerous dining and shopping possibilities in the city. In the centre you will automatically come to the large hotel "Krajina" where it is easy to get a room.

### From Negotin to Zajear                    70 km

You can continue on the main road E 771 directly from Negotin to Zaječar but it is more fun to travel along the scening route from along small, quiet roads from one village to the next. Therefore you should take the somewhat bumpy road towards the Bulgarian border. At a big cemetery on the right side you will find a sign pointing towards the route to **Kobisnica**. The pavement is in better condition again after this town. Where the road branches off to the Bulgarian Bregovo and Vidin shortly before the border, you should continue straight ahead towards Rajac and Bracevac. Continue through a small tunnel. Here the paved road becomes more narrow and much less travelled. The road runs parallel to the railroad tracks through fields and meadows, sometimes on the left, sometimes on the right. Be careful when crossing the railroad tracks: This stretch is actually in use!

Negotin

It becomes somewhat hilly between the villages of **Veljkovo** and **Rogljevo**. Turn left at the crossing in Rogljevo and continue on the very quiet and beautiful road until you reach **Rajac** which is on the right of the road on the rolling hills.

**Tip:** The sports field of the FK Rajac lies directly on this stretch. In the club house a "restoran" is also in operation.

Continue on the narrow paved road to **Bracevac**.

**Tip:** If you would like to pay the small town a visit, turn right over the small bridge, otherwise continue straight ahead.

A black and yellow sign shows the direction towards Sipikovo which is a little way uphill from here. This hilly region is more adventurous and lonelier than Vojvodina with it's endless fields. **Sipikovo** appears rather desolate. Continue through the town and over corn fields to **Mali Jasenovac**. The pavement is soon replaced by gravel and there are some steep hills to conquer. Soon you will reach the large town of **Veliki Jasenovac** where the road is paved again.

Where the road makes a right to Gradskovo, turn left. Unfortunately there are no signs. The road is somewhat hilly with several ascends and the landscape remains beautiful. After a while you will reach the small town of **Halovo** which rewards you for your hard work. Some hills are followed by a curvy downhill stretch. Afterwards the road is level from **Veliki Izvor** to Zaječar.

## Zaječar

*The city of Zaječar lies on the river Timok and has a population of about 40,000. In the centre you cannot miss the hotel Srbija-Tis where you can spend the night and also safely store your bicycle. It is really worth visiting the central square in the city which is surrounded by historical restored buildings.*

### From Zaječar to Knjaževac          65 km

**The direct connection between Zajear and Knjaževac is the main road E 771. In order to avoid traffic, there is a route through quieter areas. The following stretch is rather exhausting and the**

road is rocky at times. There are hills to conquer but you can see beautiful mountain scenery! The following stretch is very difficult to travel on in rain or fog. In this case, you should wait for better conditions!

From the city centre, follow the E 761 towards Beograd and Paracin to the edge of town where the road branches to the left towards Sljivar and Lasovo. There is a black and yellow sign in Cyrillic. The road continues uphill through the suburbs of Zaječar. Afterwards it leads somewhat down hill and then becomes level until you reach the town of Sljivar.

## Sljivar

*Here you will find very old farmhouses, some of which have deteriorated. These Balkan villages appear original and represent simpler and better days – most western European tourists cannot get enough of these sights in the beginning.*

A long hill to Lenovac follows until you reach a road to the left which leads to Leskovac and Gorna Bela Reka. Continue straight ahead for six kilometres.

Zajecar

## Lenovac

*Lenovac lies in a valley and is also very idyllic. There is a very rustic bar at the crossing. You should take a short break here and enjoy a drink!*

After the town, turn left over a bridge and again uphill, whereby there is quite an elevation to conquer. Continue downhill again to Lasovo. The landscape is very impressive here. On the left, the massive mountain range Tupiznica reaches to an elevation of 1,160 metres.

## Lasovo

*In Lasovo you will feel like you are close to the end of the world. If the sun is shining, you can admire the old houses. In rainy conditions the region can appear somewhat spooky. In any case, you should have sufficient provisions and a bicycle repair kit with you. On the left there is a small store where you can acquire some necessities.*

The road straight ahead ends somewhere in the mountains. Therefore take the road to the left at the beginning of town which leads over a bridge towards Bucje. A compact gravel and sand road follows which winds over the hill. It is very tiring but the view of the impressive mountain Tupiznica is worth it. Where the road forks in three, keep to the right and continue somewhat uphill. Various sections follow: uphill on gravel, level on sand and past mountain meadows.

At the end of this section, the road leads downhill to Bucje where you will reach a paved road that continues to the left to Knjaževac. After the tough ride on the rocky mountain section you will enjoy the downhill ride to

Knjaževac on the smooth pavement! Cross through the villages **Sokolovica**, **Lepena**, **Valevac** and **Kalicina** before you reach Knjaževac which is 18 kilometres from **Bucje**. At the beginning of town you will cross the railroad tracks and then continue straight ahead to the centre.

## Knjaževac

*The city of Knjaževac has a population of about 20,000 and numerous shopping possibilities. The guest house "Barka" at the edge of town on the road to Niš offers good overnight accomodation. The hotel in the centre was closed in the autumn of 2006, which is not unusual for a winter sports resort. The restaurant "Mali Predah" behind the bridge towards Zaječar also has rooms. You can enjoy good dining in the restaurant of the guest house "Barka". The cultural highlight is the annual Serbian Youth Cultural Festival.*

### From Knjaževac to Pirot                    65 km

From the city centre, follow the road towards Pirot. It is the shortest connection and fortunately not highly travelled. Continue on the main road towards Zaječar. After crossing the river, the road leads to the right towards Kalna and Pirot. Continue through residential areas for a while before the surroundings once again become green.

This section has very nice scenery. The first village you will reach is **Štrbac** which lies in a valley.

## Donja Kamenica

*The Manastir Svete Trojice, the convent of Holy Trinity, from 1457 lies close to Donja Kamenica.*

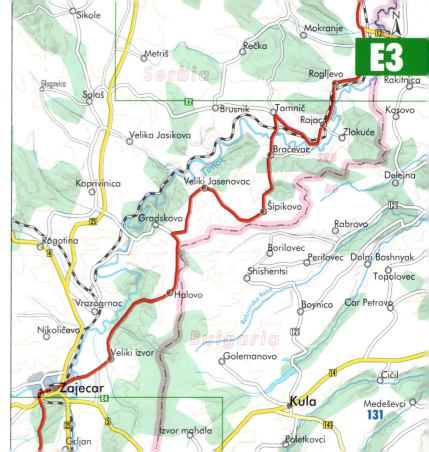

Knjaževac

The road mainly runs through the long valley which has a small uphill grade. It varies from wide to narrow. Soft hills and steep cliffs alternate. A small river runs parallel to the road.

The town of Kalna follows which is the midpoint of the stretch.

## Kalna

*Here you will find a few two-story residential houses and there are also various shopping possibilities. The hotel on the right gives a rather lonely impression. People will be amazed to see you travel by with your bicycle and it is quite* likely that they will ask in a friendly manner where you are from.

The next hill to conquer is rather poorly paved. In the autumn of 2006, the road was washed away in several locations. From the top of the hill you have a great view of the valley. Afterwards there is a downhill grade of up to 12 %. You should be very careful and watch out for the potholes. In the valley you will soon reach the town of **Cerova** followed by **Temska**. Old residential buildings line the curvy road and continue into the hills.

*Cross the river Temštica after the town. The river has washed a canyon into the rock layers on the left and is called "little Colorado". The village of* **Novi Zavoj** *is not far away. In 1963 it was flooded due to a landslide which turned the river Visoica to a lake. The 500 metre long and 50 metre high natural dam was reinforced and a hydro power plant added. The intention of the government to divert even more water from the "little Colorado" than the currently 80 percent, upset the community and therefore a decision has not yet been made.*

Landscape by Kalna

## Pirot

The entrance into Pirot is long and does not give the best impression. Factories, bus stations and fallow areas make Pirot appear unorganised. Although not very attractive, the city is interesting. There are many shopping and dining possibilities and two pizzerias by the channel. There are direct connections from the train station to Budapest, Vienna and Belgrade.

*After the city centre, the hotel block cannot be overseen. Overnight accommodation is relatively affordable in the "Pirot", the condition of the building is, however, no longer the best. If* you ask, you can take your bicycle into the building and store it near the reception.

## From Pirot to Dimitrovgrad     40 km

The stretch to Dimitrovgrad is not easy. There are three possibilities and none of them is really ideal.

The first possibility is to take the E 80 from Pirot to Dimitrovgrad. Thereby you have to travel very carefully on the edge of the road for 25 kilometres due to the high amount of traffic.

The second possibility is the big detour on the quiet street via Rsovci, Visoka Ržana and Smilovci. This route takes you over an elevation of 1,000 metres, which can hardly be accomplished in one day.

In following the description of the third possibility: Although the terrain is not easy and also leads into the mountains, the route is free of cars, not as long and very pretty.

On an access road, leave Pirot towards Dimitrovgrad and the Bulgarian border. Turn left after the railroad tracks towards Poljska Ržana and Veliko Selo. Continue on the narrow, quiet and well paved road via **Veliki** and **Mali Jovanovac** to the village of **Krupac** where you turn right at the crossing with the former petrol station. The residents will confirm the direction towards Smilovci but they will also emphasize that the section is a great challenge. Continue uphill on gravel and sand, past bushes and fields.

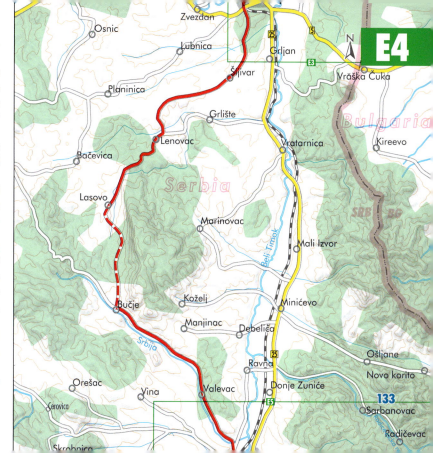

**Tip:** Note! Do not attempt to conquer this route if it is foggy, raining or generally poor weather because the roads can get very muddy. Do not forget that you are far from any tourist routes in Serbia. You should always have sufficient provisions and tools with you!

You will have to push the next three, four kilometres. The stretch is pretty steep and the road is rocky. The view however is fantastic: you can see Pirot lying nestled in the picturesque valley.

Continue on a high plateau with varying road conditions. Turn to the left at the fork in the road. Otherwise: Stay on the main road. There are hillsides, fields and bushes on both sides. Now and then you will see a sheepdog guarding a small herd of sheep and goats which you should try not to disturb. This also applies to the shepherds and the farmers that are usually armed in these remote mountain regions. If the sheepdogs begin barking at you, you should quickly make yourself recognised as a cyclist. Blind trust is not appropriate here. In such a remote

**Pirot - City centre**

area a healthy amount of carefulness and scepticism is important.

The road which is covered with hedges and thorny bushes continues for several kilometres until the landscape suddenly changes. There are fewer bushes and you will reach a high plateau which is surrounded by distant mountain ranges. The rocky, grass covered road continues straight ahead. On the left, the mountain range of the massive Vidlic reaches an elevation of 1,413 metres.

When you see the town of Odorovci in the distance on the left, you will probably be glad

to see civilisation again. Continue straight ahead and you will have to overcome several wet areas which should not be too difficult under normal weather conditions thanks to the large rocks that have been placed there. On a small paved road which has no signs, turn right and you will reach **Radejna**. The sign at the beginning of town can hardly be recognised; this is the most remote corner of Serbia.

You will have to conquer one more steep climb on the way to Dimitovgrad. Afterwards you will quickly reach the valley (be careful with the narrow curves!), which makes up for the rather exhausting stretch.

### Dimitrovgrad (Serbia)

*Like the famous Bulgarian city, the Serbian Dimitrovgrad – a centre of Bulgarian minorities – was also named after Georgi Dimitrov. It was transferred from Bulgaria to Yugoslavia after World War I. Nearly half of the population of 12,000 is Bulgarian and only 25 % is Serbian. The census from 2002 showed an unusually high portion of the population made no indication of nationality. In Dimitrovgrad you can spend the night in the hotel*

Amfora near the train station, which has direct connections to Belgrade and Sofia.

## From Dimitrovgrad (Serbia) to Dragoman (Bulgaria)
### 15 km train ride

The street route from Bulgarian Dragoman leads over the highly travelled E 80. It is more comfortable and safer the take the train for this short distance. The train travels twice daily. You can purchase tickets at the train station shortly before the arrival of the train. You must purchase the tickets for the bicycles in the train from the conductor, but normally the normal train ticket is sufficient. It is not exactly fun to get onto the train with your bicycle and to stand in the door area. The conduc-tor and customs official will complain a little but normally they look away.

The train stops in **Gradina** for at least two hours. All passports are collected and the Bulgarian border patrol takes them to a barrack. In the mean time, the customs officials check possible hiding spaces in the hallway and compartments with the help of cameras and mirrors.

## Wera Sandner and Rolf Kühnle

In the summer of 1972, Wery Sandner from Cottbus and her fiancé Rolf Kühnle from Nuremberg, whom she had met at the Black Sea, died here in the underbrush at night near the border crossing Kalotina. A single border patrol killed them with shots from his Kalashnikov. They had the intention to flee. It

was unlikely that they would risk fleeing over the Iron Curtain since their friend from West Germany had already obtained fake passports. Stefan Appelius thinks it was possible that the Stasi heard of their intentions to flee, arrested the couple at the Black Sea, brought them to the border and chased them into the brush in order to shoot them there. He says: "In the mean time we know that this happened in other cases."

Wera Sandner is buried in a cemetery near Sofia. Her fiancé's corpse was transferred to Nuremberg in 1972 and laid to rest there.

## The Iron Curtain in Bulgaria

This report is based on the research results from Dr. Stefan Appelius, who has performed research concerning the "extended wall" for many years as a professor for political science at the University of Oldenburg.

According to declarations of the Bulgarian Minister of Defence Dimitar Ludschew on February 21, 1992, at least 339 Bulgarian citizens were killed by members of the border troops. Bulgarian border troops had also killed 36 foreigners, especially tourists from the GDR, while "attempting to flee".

Dimitrovgrad - Train to Dragoman

The minister added that the documents were complete since there were no records of the years 1969, 1973, 1979 as well as for the period from 1986 to 1989. While Ludschew spoke of a "terrible crime", the Secretary for Internal Affairs Jordan Sokolow (SDS) said that the fatal shots on the demarcation line were legal and that the border troops were authorised to prevent all attempts to flee with the force of arms according to ordinance 359 from August 28, 1952.

Between 1965 and 1970, a total of 265 GDR citizens were able to flee to the west from Bulgaria since there was a rumour at that time that it was especially easy here. The number of attempts to flee increased in the following years since the inner German border became impossible to overcome as of 1971 due to the installation of spring guns.

Thousands of GDR citizens who attempted to flee via Bulgaria were put in jail. According to today's knowledge, at least 4,500 GDR citizens attempted to flee via Bulgaria. Over 80 % thereof were arrested. The arrested refugees were returned to the GDR and sentenced there. Many were bought free later by the Federal Government.

From 1944, the border to Turkey was closed off, the border to Greece could practically not be overcome from 1948. As of July 1, 1950, Bulgaria also closed off the border to Yugoslavia. The farmers living in the border area formed a "border safety protection". These civil troops were intended make it difficult for "spies" in the border area. Those who revealed a refugee were rewarded.

Restriction zones were created in the border area which could only be accessed by residents with special authorization. "Untrustworthy elements" were expelled.

There were many attempts to flee, especially on the border of the People's Republic of Bulgaria with the NATO countries Turkey and Greece. We know today that most GDR refugees were shot at the border to Greece. Fatalities were also recorded on the Turkish and Yugoslavian border. The exact number will probably never be known, also since the Bulgarians buried killed refugees in the restriction zone. In the beginning this also applied to the victims from the GDR until the protests of East German parents lead to a secret agreement between the GDR embassy and the Bulgarian Attorney General that the killed GDR citizens were to at least be buried in a cemetery.

At the end of the 1950's, about one third of Bulgaria was a "prohibited zone" which could not be accessed by foreigners. Already before the declaration of the firing order in 1952, according to official records, members of the border troops had shot at least 172 Bulgarians while attempting to flee. In 1953, the community in Sofia passed an amendment to

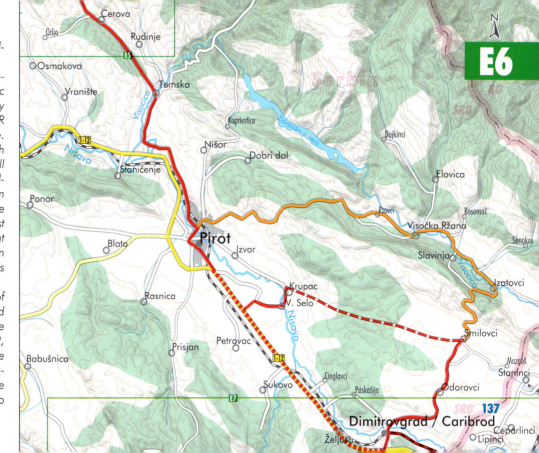

the Criminal Code, making illegal exiting of the People's Republic punishable by death.

The case of the 42 year old electrician, Gospodinow, was documented. He was arrested in 1949 while attempting to flee and sentenced to prison. In early August 1962, he was sentenced to death for "damaging a telephone line" and executed.

The border to Greece and Turkey was closed off by a 15 kilometre wide restriction zone and could only be accessed with special authorization. The access to this zone was characterised by warning signs and barriers and was protected by armed soldiers. The warning signs were displayed in Bulgarian and German. There were no mines or spring guns on the Bulgarian border but instead a raked border strip which was lined by a three metre high fence. This was two kilometres before the official border. Within the border facilities, fire was usually opened on refugees without warning.

The Bulgarian border regime also did not change after the European good neighbour policy was signed with Greece (1973) and Tur-

**Bread sales on roadside in Kruscha**

key (1975). Those who wanted to flee to these countries had to expect death. The Bulgarian border troops received rewards: the arrest of a GDR citizen paid five days of holiday, and they received ten days for shooting one.

Frank Schachtschneider, a 26 year old electrician from Berlin-Köpernick, was suffering from a life threatening head injury when he was admitted to hospital in Bourgas in August 1988. According to the official description, he had been shot in the head. The autopsy however showed that his skull had been bashed during his arrest by the border

soldiers. An examination of the "incident" by the military police in Sliwen was immediately stopped.

In early July 1989, Michael Weber, a 19 year-old student from Leipzig, was killed near the border to Greece. The counsellor of the Federal German embassy, who dealt with the murder of the young man upon order of the Federal Government, found "the possibility that he was robbed after death could not be ruled out". It was stated in the internal communication of the consular departments of the GDR embassy in Sofia: "According to the autopsy report, the shot was fired from above at a short distance, which qualifies as a targeted and intended fatal shot." The proceedings against the offender, a soldier of the same age, were stopped in 1994. He was not sentenced despite compelling evidence.

## Dragoman

In Dragoman, continue straight ahead from the train station to the end of the road. Turn left there and right where the restaurant is. A small paved road runs parallel to the highway to Sofia. A sign indicated a newly constructed family hotel. There is no other overnight accommodation in Dragoman. A double room costs € 15 per night and the owner also sells cold beverages.

## From Dragoman to Tran — 41 km

The stretch to the popular health resort in the south is not that simple. The lack of signs makes things quite difficult. It is important to be alert for the following kilometres, to read the signs carefully and to pay particular attention at the road crossings. In Serbia most of the signs are in Cyrillic and Latin script, but here in the Bulgarian province you will only find Cyrillic. The signs are often rusty and hard to read.

From the hotel in Dragoman, travel a short distance in the direction you came from, turn left into the road and continue to the west towards Gaber. You will soon leave the city behind you on a quiet, paved road.

If you ask someone for directions, you should keep in mind that nodding and shaking your head has the opposite meaning

In Grabesevci

than what you are accustomed to in Western Europe. When a Bulgarian shakes their head, it is hard to know if they are adapting to the foreigner or not. In any case, you should listen carefully: "da" = "yes", "ne" = "no".

The street to Gaber leads through a big valley. It is surrounded on all sides by mountains and hills.

## Gaber

In Gaber you will come to a blue sign which shows Tran to the right. Continue on this road with beautiful scenery until you reach Kruscha. The signs are very difficult to read.

**Tip:** Here and in the other Bulgarian border areas you will occasionally find border patrols which will ask for your passport and want to know where you are going. They will study your papers carefully, they might make a phone call, but there will be no problems.

## Kruscha

*The small Bulgarian towns near the border to Serbia are partially in a shocking condition. The few stores are nearly empty and if you are lucky, you will find a fresh loaf of white bread for one Lei, which is about 50 cents. You can find one such store in Kruscha on the right side. The bread is usually brought with a car and sold directly from the trunk.*

**Tip: The village dogs are bothersome which start barking already from the distance. Luckily, most of the dogs are behind a fence.**

The road becomes narrower after Kruscha and leads you uphill. Continue through pine and leaf forests with a view into the lonely valleys. Then the forest opens again and you con-

In the centre of Tran

tinue over grassy high plateaus. Cross through the town of **Vrabcha**, which appears in a sorry state, and continue downhill past jagged cliffs to the 63 which is wider and leads from **Breznik** to Tran. Keep to the right towards Tran and the spectacular chasm of the river Erma.

## Tran

*In the middle of Tran, you will find all the important buildings: stores, a bank, a post office and a Gostiniza (a hotel). In a Magasin (store) on the right side, you can exchange Euro for Leva,* which is curiously not possible at the post office or bank. If you do not want to take the long journey to Kyustendil, you can spend the night in Tran since you will only find lonely villages in remote areas between Tran and Kyustendil. If you have brought a tent, it is possible to camp near one of the small villages. However, if you need a roof, you need to make good evaluation of the conditions and the weather.

## From Tran to Kyustendil          65 km

Continue a small distance on the main road towards Serbia, Strezimitovci and Surdulica. Turn left on the road to Vukan (Cyrillic Bykan). You will make good progress on the six kilometres to Vukan.

On the right side in the lonely field in the valley you will soon see a massive memorial. A figure stands in front of two massive concrete blocks, which appears to have broken through a wall. Vulkan lies on the left. Continue straight ahead until you reach Kosturinci.

You will occasionally find a sign which leads towards Dilga Luka/alga Luka. In any case, continue on the road towards Dilga Luka!

In **Kosturinci** you will find a nice little church, but otherwise there is no reason to stop. You will make good progress through the beautiful mountain scenery to **Dolna Melna**. In the small store you can buy the most important things. A clay coloured church stands on a hill. There is a half rusted sign on a fence which confirms that you are heading in the right direction: Trekljano 15 kilometres.

The road narrows and becomes lonelier. High bushes

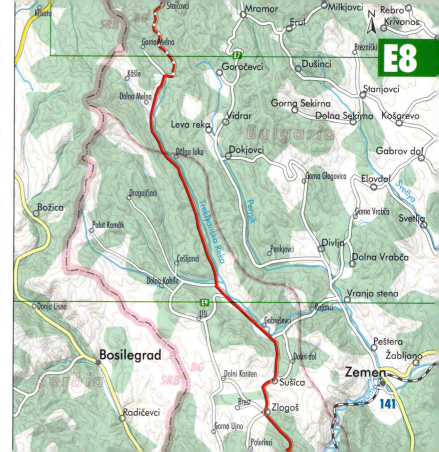

accompany part of the gravel road which leads you to a remote valley where you will find the small town of Dilga Luka.

## Dilga Luka

*It is mostly abandoned – rotten barns and houses line the hill. The next village of Kosovo is nearly completely abandoned. Fields, forests and soft hills dominate the landscape.*

The surface of the pavement varies and you will hardly see anyone.

This changes in Trekljano: you are back in civilisation.

## Trekljano

*The village is larger than the previous ones. There are large buildings with peppers hanging to dry in the windows. On the right you will find a nice store where you can take a rest on the wooden benches.*

**Tip: You should probably have a good meal here: It is about 40 kilometres until you reach Kyustendil.**

Continue on the smooth pavement until you reach **Gabreschevci**. Turn right there towards Kyustendil. **Sushitsa** and **Zlogosch** are the next villages on the route which are

Kyustendil

characterised by fields, hills and occasional birches. Continue downhill to **Dragovischtica** where Kyustendil is clearly signposted. You still have 11 kilometres to get through. You must once again conquer a hill. From the top you will see your destination in the distance in the valley. After **Sovoljano** the route continues downhill. You then simply roll into Kyustendil.

The first suburbs of the city are not very inviting. Abandoned areas and industrial grounds line both sides of the road. The city centre however has positive surprises. Cross the highway E 871, which leads to Sofia, and continue straight ahead to the centre.

**Tip: Not far from the main square you will find the hotel "Bulgaria" where you can spend the night for little money. A double room costs about € 15 per night without breakfast.**

## Kyustendil

*This city has a population of 50,300 and has an elevation of 525 metres. It is on the western edge of Bulgaria. It is 27 kilometres linear distance to the border triangle of Bulgaria, Serbia and Macedonia. The Osogovo Mountain lies to the west with an elevation of over 2,000 metres. Kyustendil is a well-known health spa in the most southern part of the fertile valley. There are numerous shopping and dining possibilities in the city.*

*Apart from the reasonably priced hotel "Bulgaria", you can also choose between the hotel "Belbadsh" (across from the train station), the hotel "Pautalia" (on main square) and the hotel "Chissarlka" (in the park). There are direct connections to Sofia from the train station.*

## Return to Germany

If you continue towards Macedonia, Greece and the Black Sea, it is recommended to take the train from Kyustendil to Sofia. This connection is served several times daily and bicycles can be taken on board the train without problems. The trip costs about € 5. The addition for the bicycle is paid on the train. In the capital you will arrive at the Sofia Central Gara.

Hotels are fairly expensive here. You can get a double room in the Residence Hotel in the city centre for about € 85. Other hotels are significantly more expensive.

There is only one airport bus which allows bicycles. You must purchase a second ticket in advance at the counter for the bicycle and stamp it in the bus! The bus driver can be unfriendly, but there is plenty of room in the bus to the airport.

At the airport, the bicycle must be as compact as possible, the air taken out of the tires and the bicycle is packed in red foil afterwards. Now it can be checked in as bulky luggage. The Bulgarian airline Hemus Air does not charge extra for bicycles. This however can change.

921 km

*At the train station in Kyustendil*

## From Kyustendil to Blagoevgrad            **60 km**

The arrival is as described with the plane to Sofia, and from there with regional transportation to Kyustendil. But maybe you already have completed the previously described stages and are continuing your journey from here.

From the centre of town, follow the road to the east towards Dupnica. At the edge of town it branches to the right before a bridge and leads you through a desolate landscape which is quiet and smooth. On the horizon you will see the foothills of the Rila Mountain

145

*Pastuh - St. Ivan Church*

which is the highest peak of the Balkan with an elevation of 2,925 metres.

Continue through the towns of **Piperkov Chiflik** and **Bagrentsi** on a long alley of poplars until you reach **Novi Chiflik**. After **Nevestino**, which is larger than the previous towns, turn right towards Blagoevgrad.

*Shortly afterwards you will encounter 500 years of history: cross the 100 metre long Kadin Bridge over the Struma from the year 1470.*

**Tip:** The restaurant on the right of the bridge is named after the Struma. It is 48 kilometres from here to Blagoevgrad.

Surrounded by mountain ranges, fields and fruit orchards dominate the landscape. The windy road forks at Chetirtsi. Turn left here towards Blagoevgrad. The valley becomes narrower. To the right there is a cliff, on the left the lively river. After several kilometres with impressive scenery, you will reach the interesting mountain village of Pastuh.

## Pastuh

*Small houses built of stones follow the rolling hillside and a few nice restaurants invite you to take a break. The small chapel of St. Ivan which lies behind the village was constructed in the typical style of the 15th and 17th century and is well worth a visit.*

## Boboshevo

*Where the valley becomes somewhat wider, you will find the city of Boboshevo in the middle of a region that has been populated for at least 7,000 years which has been proven by excavations in Slatino which is two kilometres further. From the 15th to the 17th century, the city was a religious and cultural centre with an abundance of churches and monasteries. The most well known today is the St. Dimitri*

*monastery which is also very significant in the history of architecture. The completely painted church was built in 1488 after the destruction by the Ottomans. The cloister however already existed in the 10th century. It is not only popular because this is where Ivan Rilski (Johannes von Rila) began his life as a monk before he moved to a hermit cave further to the west at Skrino and then formed the also famous cloister Rila ten kilometres east of Boboshevo with his followers.*

From the centre of town, follow a gravel road to **Dragodan**, where you will come to a

*Boboshevo*

paved road which you follow to the left for 200 metres.

Tip: At the fork in the road to Blagoevgrad there are two alternatives:

## Alternative 1:

Turn left over the railroad tracks and the Struma towards **Kocherinovo**. From here you can travel straight ahead to the Rila cloister. If you would like to avoid the 7 kilometre long detour, turn right onto the E 79 and continue until you turn left towards Blageovgrad. There are slight hills to conquer on this route and you must pay attention to the traffic before you use the wide strip on the side of the road.

## Alternative 2:

This route leads through small villages with sections of poor road conditions. You first travel on a smooth, quiet paved road to **Borovez** and **Buranovo** through the friendly landscape which is dominated by fields, meadows and fruit trees. Continue to **Krumovo**. At the village square, a compact sandy road branches to the left. It leads you over 7 kilometres through the small villages of **Buchino** and **Balgarchevo** to **Zelendol** and is somewhat adventurous. At times you will have to dismount and push. Afterwards you will make good progress to Blagoevgrad.

### Blagoevgrad

*Blagoevgrad, the capital of Bulgarian Macedonia, has a population of 76,000 and is one of the largest cities in the southwest of Bulgaria. It is an important regional administrative centre. It is also recognised as a health spa with 30 mineral*

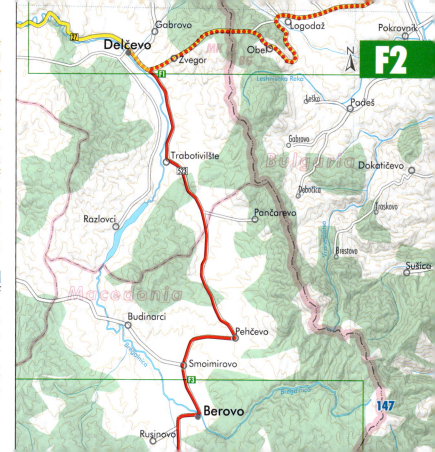

*Bumpy road by Blagoevgrad*

springs. The city was created on the old Thrace settlement Skaptopara, as stated in a document from 238. Nothing is known about the medieval development. During the Ottoman period, it was called Cuma-ı Bala and later partially translated into Gorna Dzhumaja. The strategically important fortification developed in the middle of the 18th/beginning of the 19th century to a large trade and industrial centre. The district of Varosha, which developed during the refounding of Bulgaria, is well maintained with typical constructions. The pedestrian area offers an abundance of restaurants, cafés and boutiques.

Since 1950, the city carries the name of the founder of the Bulgarian Communist Party (1919), Dimitar Blagoev (1856-1924).

You can spend the night in the two-star hotel "Rio". Also available is the hotel "Alen Mak" on the main square. Two kilometres to the north on the road to Sofia you will also find the hotel "Bor" and the motel "Rilzi". There are direct connections to Sofia and Thessaloniki from the train station.

## From Blagoevgrad (Bulgaria) to Berovo (Macedonia)                    80 km

The road to Macedonia leads to the west through **Zelendol**, **Selishte** and **Logodazh** to the border crossing Delchevski Prohod at an elevation of 1,085 metres. In Selishte, you can enjoy a cup of coffee in a small store on the left side. After Logodazh, when the route turns to the south for a while, you can enjoy a beautiful view of the valley to the left and the distant Rila Mountain. The road continues with many curves and there is a small and difficult stretch that is difficult before you reach the border to Macedonia.

The control at the border between Bulgaria and Macedonia is without difficulties and the border officers are friendly.

## The history of Macedonia

Only the southern portion of this part of the former republic of Yugoslavia belonged to the Kingdom of Macedonia in the ancient world. As of the 9th century, it became part of the first Bulgarian Empire. In the 11th century, Bulgaria lost power in the region to the Byzantine Empire, was however able to regain it in 1205 in the Battle of Adrianople from the Latin Byzantine Empire. In the middle of the 14th century, the

Serbian kingdom under Stefan Uroš IV Dušan, conquered the entire region of Macedonia with the exception of Thessaloniki and its immediate surroundings. He was only able to maintain it for a short time before the Byzantines ruled again. It was then gradually conquered by the Ottoman Empire. In 1392, the Turks conquered Skopje which they renamed Üsküp. From the beginning of the 15th century until 1912, the area of today's Macedonia belonged to the Ottoman Empire.

After the end of the Balkan Wars (1912/ 1912), the region of Macedonia between Greece, Serbia and Bulgaria was divided. The Serbian portion belonged to the Kingdom of the Serbs, Croats and Slovenes from 1918-1941, which was called the Kingdom of Yugoslavia as of 1929. There was an exchange of Turkish Muslims and Greek refugees in the Greek portion after World War I. As a result thereof, most parts of this region speak Greek today.

During World War II, the area was occupied by Bulgaria after 1941 which was fought against by a Partisan movement. The communist Partisans of Yugoslavia recognised the existence of an independent (Slavic) Macedonian nation for the first time in 1943. In 1946, the region Vardar-Macedonia (southern Serbia) was declared to be the sixth constituent republic of the Yugoslavian state (SR Makedonija).

After the collapse of Yugoslavia in 1991, the constituent republic of Macedonia declared independence and was accepted by the United Nations in 1993 under the English name of Former Yugoslav Republic of Macedonia (FY-ROM). This also meant recognition by most of the EU states. In December 2005, Macedonia was granted the status of an EU candidate. The acceptance of the Former Yugoslav Republic of Macedonia into NATO was opposed by Greece in 2008 due to the name conflict.

The uphill climb is worth it. Continue on the Macedonian side on a smooth, quiet road for six kilometres down hill until you reach the town of **Zvegor**, where the houses line the soft hillside. At the end of town, make a left into the road to Berovo.

**Tip:** If you would like to view Delchevo, continue straight ahead and then return to this spot afterwards. The small town with a population of 10,500, which was named after the revolutionary hero Gotse Delchev, offers various shopping and dining possibilities.

The road to Berovo is very quiet and smooth and leads through a wide valley. You will see corn fields, grazing land and small fruit orchards. At a distance to the right you will see the Golak Mountain with an elevation of 1,536 metres.

At the branch to **Trabotiviste**, it is still a further 28 kilometres to Berovo. The landscape becomes hillier, the wide valley gradually becomes narrower and there is a slight uphill grade to conquer to **Pekhchevo**, which lies somewhat to the left of the route. Continue through **Chiflik** and afterwards somewhat downhill through the small town of **Smoimirovo** until you reach Berovo. On the left you will see a petrol station and a shop. To the right leads you to Strumica and straight ahead to the centre of town.

## Berovo

The little city in eastern Macedonia lies at an elevation of about 900 metres and has a population of 14,000. The lake of the same name lies to the southeast and is a popular tourist attraction. The wooden artistic products are as well known as the Berovo cheese. There is a hotel, a museum, an old church, banks and numerous shopping possibilities.

## From Berovo to Strumica                40 km

There is quite a bit of elevation to conquer on the next stretch, but the road is little travelled and in good condition. Continue uphill to the south through fields and meadows. The road winds through the mountains of Macedonia and the scenery is nice. The valley occasionally becomes narrower and you will pass forest areas and cliffs. Later it becomes wider again and fields and meadows dominate the landscape in which individual houses and small villages are tucked away.

After several ups and downs you will suddenly come across a bizarre sight: a small white merry-go-round behind a fence with a large white sign on it.

**Tip: From here the road becomes steep! You have to conquer the Prevedena Pass**

*Memorial on the 1,394 metre high Palazlija*

with an elevation of 1,167 metres. Make sure that you have plenty of beverages and food with you since shopping possibilities are very rare in this lonely region. Continue up the hill with an eight to ten percent grade.

At the top of the pass you will be greeted by a metal sign full of bullet holes. It is somewhat uncomfortable to be reminded of the Balkan Wars this way – a rusty old bus only adds to the melancholy.

Continue down to the valley with a downhill grade of ten percent but: Be careful – the curves can be very tight! The small town at the bottom of the valley offers dining and shopping possibilities which are also open Sundays, providing cyclists with the important necessities. Individual houses line the hills and you can put up a tent on one of the large fields.

The road once again leads you uphill with an eleven percent grade. The **Palazlija** Pass with an elevation of 1,394 metres awaits you with a large stone memorial. There is also an information plaque and a map of the region. The border between the regions Berovo and Strumica runs along the crest.

From here it is a long ride into the Strumica Valley. You will be rewarded for the burdens. You will have a beautiful view of the small plain into which the roads winds.

**Tip: Watch our for the sharp curves! At various locations you can take a break and enjoy the view.**

The structure of the fields can be recognised, the settlements and the greenhouses. Fruit orchards, vineyards, peppers and corn dominate the picture.

After several kilometres downhill, you will reach **Petralinci** in the plain with its small white church. Shortly afterwards you will come to **Dabilja** where you will come to a fork in the road. Five kilometres to the right is Strumica and the river of the same name.

## Strumica

You will be surprised by the liveliness of the town after the rather quiet Berovo. The town has a population of 55,000. The region is of great historical importance. The first settlements already existed here at around 7,000 B.C.. Since the 9th century A.D., the city belonged to the Bulgarian Empire for several centuries until it was conquered by the Ottomans in 1395. In 1912 it was reincorporated into Bulgaria after six centuries of Turkish rule, was however soon surrendered to Serbia/Yugoslavia.

The economy of the city is now based on the production and trade of textiles. The region is considered to be one of the wealthiest in Macedonia and it is no surprise that it also has an active night life, which is particularly in the Lebljebedzijska Straße

### From Strumica (Macedonia) to Petric (Bulgaria)        53 km

First, turn back to **Dabilja**, then turn right towards Robovo, Murino and Bansko.

Continue on the quiet road through the valley with many fields and meadows. On the right you will see the Belasica Mountain, on the left the Ograzden Mountain.

Continue through the small village of **Robovo** with individual buildings, large gardens and adjacent fields. Somewhat hidden you can see small church tower.

F3

151

**Murtino** is quite similar. Between the towns you will occasionally see trucks which transport the vegetables from the greenhouses.

The Belsica mountain range slowly comes closer and also the border between Macedonia and Greece. The road becomes somewhat hilly and winds along the foothills of the mountains. Individual houses are built high in the hills.

You will reach **Kolesino** and a short time later **Mokrievo**. Turn left towards Novo Selo which is situated on the main road to Bulgaria, past Strumica. Straight ahead leads you to Mokrievo. Afterwards the road becomes a poorly maintained trail, which disappears into the hills. In **Novo Selo** you will find a few stores.

Follow the main road to the east to the border crossing between Macedonia and Bulgaria, which you will pass right after **Novo Konjarevo**. The road continues uphill in Bulgaria. At the highest point, you can take a break at Samuil's Fortress.

## Samuil's Fortress

*It was built by the Bulgarian Tsar between 1009 and 1014 and is today a cultural memorial within a museum park. Tsar Samuil is*

Strumica

*considered a national hero although he lost the decisive battle against the Byzantine Empire (Battle of Kleidion, 1014) five kilometres further to the south in Kljutch (key), which confirmed the independence of Bulgaria. The Byzantine Emperor Basileios II apparently sent 14,000 prisoners of war home blinded, which caused Samuil to have a heart attack.*

Continue downhill and soon you will have a view similar to that of the plains on the Macedonian side: Vegetable fields at the foot of a mountain range.

## Petric

*The Bulgarian city of Petric lies at the foot of the Belasica mountain range and has a population of about 35,000. During the Middle Ages, it was an important fortification in the battle against the Byzantine Empire. Today it is a centre for the processing of tobacco, fruits and fruits and vegetables. There are several dining and shopping possibilities. You can spend the night in the hotel "Bulgaria" or in the hotel "Elena" which lie close together. A double room in the hotel "Bulgaria" costs about 44 Leva in the autumn of 2006. There are direct connections to Sofia from the train station.*

## From Petrich to Goce Delchev            50 km

The main road 198 towards Kulata has new, good pavement and some traffic. Apart from the numerous vineyards after Petrich, the landscape appears somewhat desolate. You will notice that there is a lot of plastic rubbish in the fields and meadows.

After a few kilometres you will see an old sign at the beginning of Drangovo inviting

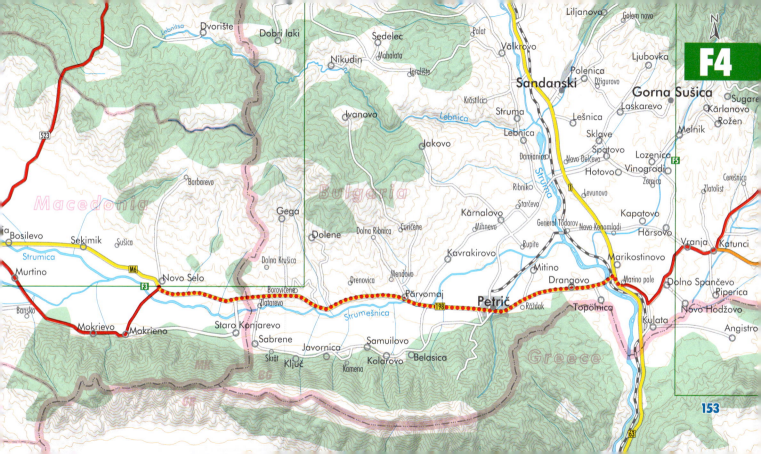

you to the restaurant "Tumbite". Cross the river Struma and you will reach the crossing with the E 79. Do not (!) orient yourself towards Kulata, which lies near the border to Greece, but rather cross under the road in a right curve and remain on the 198 which leads to Katunci and Goce Delchev.

The next village that you will reach is **Marino Pole**, which appears to be very Greek: Vineyards, small fields and numerous goat herds. On the mountains in the distance you will see a few windmills.

Tip: Watch out for the potholes!

Tip: In Marino Pole you can spend the night in the very modern and clean Kompleks Komitite. A double room costs € 32. There is also a huge swimming pool in the grounds.

In **Chuchuligovo** the road forks. Keep to the left towards Katunci and Goce Delchev. On a narrow paved road with several potholes you will cross through **Dolno Spanchevo** and continue slightly uphill to **Vranja** where the road continues to the right. In the centre of **Katunci** you will find the hotel "Liapchev". At

Petric

the end of town, there is a petrol station where you can eat.

Continue 27 kilometres on the paved route with little traffic until you reach **Goce Delchev**. Follow the signs to Goce Delchev. In the beginning the road leads slightly uphill, then level, and then continuously uphill. The road is curvy and has potholes. After ten kilometres, continue downhill into **Gorno Spanchevo**. From the nearby hill, old ruins greet you.

It is a good idea to stock up on drinks here since ahead of you lies a long climb to the top of the Popski Pass, which has an elevation of

1,120 metres. Continue on the smooth pavement which has recently been repaired. The curvy stretch first leads you through a forest of leaf trees, then later you have an impressive view. At times the road leads along steep cliffs, so be very careful! Now and then there are sharp rocks on the road! If it is rainy, parts of this stretch can be foggy and you can expect the first snow in October.

The last part before reaching the top of the pass is very exhausting, but at the top there are several dining possibilities and you can also find overnight accommodation. In amongst some pine and spruce trees you will for example find the "Tikihijat Kut" on the left side. A few metres further on the right you will find the hotel "Bulgartabak". The wooden plateau with the guesthouses and hotels is very idyllic despite the bronze soldiers on the left of the road, and invites you to take a longer break.

From the small plateau, continue on the winding road into the valley of the Mesta river. The surface of the road is not as good as the ascend to the pass, however it is quite good to travel on. Shortly before you reach **Dobrotino**

By Petric

you will have a fantastic view! The town lies somewhat away from the road. At a bus stop, where cows commonly graze, you can park your bike and walk up a little hill in order to view the church there. You will reach Goce Delchev on the main road from Dobrotino.

## Goce Delchev

*The city greets you with buildings, which have no laster on the outside, but has a rather pleasant, well-kept image in the centre. It lies surrounded by massive mountain ranges in a long valley and has a population of about 24,000.*

In the Slavjanka Mountains

Similar to Delchevo in Macedonia, this city was also named after the revolutionary hero (Goce = Georgi) in 1951. Until then it was called Nevrokop. Nearby excavations of the Romanic city Nikopolis ad Nestrum from the 2nd century were starde, but had to be discontinued for financial reasons.

Goce Delchev is an insider tip in the region. The vicinity to the Pirin National Park and the well kept city centre make it an attractive stopover. The shopping road in the small centre is nice for a stroll. Numerous stores, snack bars and cafés make this an enjoyable stay for any visitor. You can spend the night in the hotel "Nevrokop" in the centre, next to the park and a chruch.

## From Goce Delchev to Dospat                    50 km

Continue to the east on a smooth, paved road with some traffic through the level valley landscape. Cross over the Mesta river and after 9 kilometres you will reach the small village of **Debnica**. The wooded mountains lie ahead of you and soon the road begins to ascend. To the left, there are pine forests, to the right you can enjoy beautiful views. Further up, the landscape becomes more open and you will reach Dolno Drjanovo, which lies on a hillside.

### Dolno Drjanovo

You will find two mosques in the centre of town, with white minarets, which reach to the sky. Rustic cafés on the main road invite you to take a break. This is Pomakish land, the region of the Bulgarian speaking Muslims.

Continue up and down through the pine forests. In open areas you will often see pallets with sandstone and slate from the

Goce Delchev

surrounding quarries. At the turn towards Pletena, you will cross a small river in an idyllic valley before continuing uphill to **Satovcha** which is not a very inviting sight due to its with dilapidated houses. Half of the stretch is behind you now. Over rolling hills with fields, birches and pine forests, continue until you reach Dospat.

### Dospat

Dospat is also on a hillside and the minaret of a mosque dominates the image of the city, which appears somewhat unstructured with multi-story buildings. In the past years, the

town at an elevation of 1,200 metres and a mostly Pomakish population of about 3,000, has increasingly won importance as a tourist destination. You can spend the night in the three star hotel "Diamant" or in the hotel "Panorama" which is a little further out of town or in the hotel restaurant "Ribarska Srechta".

The Dospat Lake is not far away, one of the biggest dammed lakes in Bulgaria. It accumulates water from the river of the same name. There are numerous recreational accommodations around the lake and it is a very popular destination for tourists and water sports enthusiasts.

### From Dospat to Smoljan                    75 km

Devin and Smoljan are signposted from the centre of Dospat. Continue slightly uphill through mixed pine and spruce forests. The condition of the road surface is reasonable and there is not too much traffic, like everywhere in the region.

After several kilometres you will reach a hilly mountain meadow at Zmeica where an

*In Dolno Drjanovo*

old Roman stone-arched bridge leads over a stream.

The windy road continues up and down hill and then finally leads down a steep hill to **Borino**. The hotel and restaurant "Chabana"

on the right side is a fairly new construction. The AMT petrol station serves coffee.

You will often have good views in the open landscape. The town of Teshel is beautiful with a small reservoir in the middle of the mountains. A breath taking stretch through a chasm leads to Jagodina on the right. The rustic hotel and restaurant "Orfei" lies next to a stream close to **Teshel** between the cliffs.

With the reservoir on the right, you will reach the town of **Grohotno** after five kilometres on a partially washed out road where a mosque reaches above the other buildings. A narrow valley closes in, lined by cliffs and accompanied by a stream. The town of **Nastan** lies impressively surrounded by steep cliffs. You can enjoy a reasonably priced meal at a snack bar. The favourite of the locals is a light cabbage broth with bread. It tastes somewhat sour and will probably not be to every visitor's taste.

Shortly after Nastan you will come to a fork in the road.

**Tip:** Four kilometres to the left you will find the health spa Devin.

Turn right towards Smoljan. On the grounds of a fish farm you will find a hotel with restaurant: "Ribirskata Chija". About 16 kilometres after Nastan you will reach Shiroka Laka.

## Shiroka Laka

*The village is known for it's houses typical for the Rhodopes, which line the hillsides. After the thick, white walls you will find a small garden with a drinking fountain. The nearly 600 Greek Orthodox residents have two churches, one of which, the Holy Mother of God, has an iconostasis worth visiting. The town is also known for the Rhodopes music. Several of the most famous singers are from here and there is a school for folk music and instruments.*

It is five kilometres from Shiroka Laka to **Vodata**. Possibly after dining in the Greek restaurant, continue to the right towards Smoljan, which is uphill. Travel through a popular winter sport and hiking region where numerous hotels and restaurants are under construction in the mountains. You still have about 20 kilometres ahead of you, which are very exhausting! The reward is a curvy downhill stretch into Smoljan.

Dospat Lake

At the beginning of Smoljan, you will find the hotel "Eserata" next to a pond. But you still are not at the bottom! Continue through some very sharp curves. Smoljan stretches over several kilometres and it is best to follow the signs to Madan.

## Smoljan

*The city is the highest in Bulgaria with an elevation of about 1,000 metres. Nearly 32,000 people have settled here in the valley of the rivers Cherna (Black) and Bjela (White) in the Rhodope mountains.*

*After 500 years of Ottoman rule, it was freed in 1912 and in 1960, three communities got together to form a modern city. It is worth paying a visit to the churches Sweti Georgie and Wissarion Smoljanski, the second largest cathedral of the country. There is also a historical museum, an art gallery, the shopping area of the copper traders and numerous houses from the time of the Bulgarian revival.*

*There are several dining and shopping possibilities. You can spend the night in the hotels "Ribkata" and "Kiparis".*

### From Smoljan to Zlatograd                    38 km

Smoljan partly has an industrial appearance but on the eastern edge of town there are some really nice parts. At the square where you will find a large supermarket, turn right towards Madan and Kardzali. The city stretches over a longer distance and then turns into the town of **Vlahovo**. Continue through a very picturesque valley. On the right you will be accompanied by a river and there is little traffic on the good pavement. In the small town of **Podvis** you will find a store on the right. After the very small village of **Robino** you will reach Taran with its white mosque. In Taran you can purchase supplies.

You will soon pass a check point of the Bulgarian Border Police where you will most likely be checked. The border police will check your entrance stamp very carefully and ask where you are from and where you are going.

You will come to a fork in the road about five kilometres after **Taran**: turn right towards Zlatograd and Madan, pass Srednogorci, and you will arrive in Madan after seven kilometres.

## Madan

*The city with a population of 7,000 was founded by ore miners. The region has been known for its lead ores since the 5th century B. C. The majority is Islamic and a mosque dominates the main square.*

*You can spend the night in the hotel "Korona" or in "Urap". This hotel is easy to find with its nine floors. There are also restaurants, cafés and a small market.*

It is a further 16 kilometres to Zlatograd. The largest hills have been conquered and

Stop in Madan

the roads become flatter, however there is still some elevation to be conquered. You will come to the highest point on the Madan-Zlatograd stretch, where the road branches off the right towards Strashimir. At the top you have an open view and can take a break in a waiting shelter.

On the perfect pavement, continue downhill on the curvy road through the small town of **Tsatsarovtsi**. You should check your brakes in advance since there are parts without guardrails and some of the curves are very sharp!

Once you have reached the bottom, you will be greeted by a light-coloured obelisk instead of a normal town sign.

## Zlatograd

*Zlatograd in the Rhodope Mountains is the most southern city in Bulgaria and has a population of about 9,000. The Varbica river runs through it. The constructions, memorials and lanterns on the main square near the river appear quite monumental and give the city a somewhat codl appearance. There is an Ethnographic Complex and a watermill, which serves as a museum. To the east lies the reservoir named after the city. There are various hotels where you can spend the night.*

### From Zlatograd to Momcilgrad/Kardzhali    70 km

From the most southern city of Bulgaria, continue towards Momcilgrad. In the beginning, the road runs parallel to the river Varbica. The road leads you slightly uphill on good pavement. Continue through wooded, hilly terrain. After about 9 kilometres you will reach the town of **Preseka** where you will find a very small mosque.

Turn left at Preseka towards the towns of Dobrintsi, General Geshevo, Ustrem and Dzebel. You will reach the town of **Dobrintsi** after about 4 kilometres. The road continues uphill through **General Geshevo** until you reach **Ustren**. After Ustren, cross a small river twice and soon the road leads you downhill again. Continue on the road until you reach **Mrezicko**. After this town, you will first pass the road to Kozica on the right and then later also the road to Rogozce on the right. Continue straight ahead until you reach the city of Dzebel.

Cross the river at **Dzebel** and you will reach the unusual centre. From here, continue to the northeast on the main road which connects the cities of Kardzali and Momcilgrad. First you will reach the town of **Vilkovic** and later the very small village of **Plazishte**. A sign follows which indicates that there are a further 10 kilometres until Kardzali. On a slightly hilly and quiet road, you will come to a location, which is signposted as "Danger Zone".

**Tip:** You have the choice on the main road: Either you continue to the right to-

*On the road towards Kardzali*

wards Momcilgrad and Krumovgrad, or you turn left and make a 9 kilometre detour to the interesting city Kardzali on the Studen Kladenec lake. The centre can be reached via a bridge.

## Kardzali

*The city lies on both sides of the river Arda between the reservoirs Kardzhali (w) and Studen Kladenec (e). The region has been populated since the Neolithic period and the historical museum has an abundance of findings. The name originates from a Turkish leader who conquered the area in the 14th century. As a result, it was almost exclusively populated by Turks who felt cornered by the Bulgarians after World War I. With the political changes of 1989, strong nationalist movements as well as the desolate economic situation led to the situation that many Turks felt forced to emigrate to Turkey. Nevertheless of the 50,000 people living here 62 percent are still Turks.*

*The tobacco industry in the region has stagnated due to the abundance of ore and the metallurgy. Positive developments are also expected in the tourism sector. The Thracian city of Perperikon lies 15 kilometres to the northeast, embedded in a cliff. It is the largest megalithic finding in the Balkans. The artificial cave of Nenkovo in the northwest, which was discovered in 2001, is compared with Stonehenge with its potential astronomic meaning, or with the Newgrange in Ireland, since a ray of sunlight passes through a slit in the rock on one single day in the year and illuminates the back of the cave.*

*The historical museum from 1910 is similar to an Oriental madrasah (Quran school) and*

*is also worth paying a visit to. The monastery of John the Baptist from the 11th century has been so thoroughly renovated that it nearly lost its original character. The clock is unique: Every hour it plays the Bulgarian Revolutionary Hymn.*

*In the centre of Kardzali, you can stay at the hotel Ustra for a reasonable price, double rooms start from € 26. The hotel Ustra is in the General Delov 1. There are numerous dining and shopping possibilities. The centre has some city flair and you can have a beer in a lively bistro or pub and mingle with the locals. If the weather is good, you can take a walk along the shores of the lake and relax. There are direct connections to Dimitrovgrad from the train station.*

After the detour to Kardzali, continue on the main road back towards Momcilgrad and Krumovgrad. The distance between the centres of the two towns is 16 kilometres.

## Momcilgrad

*Momcilograd lies 16 kilometres south of Kardzhali, is significantly smaller and of a very different structure. There are parking facilities*

Church in Momcilgrad

*in the centre and a few cafés, but in general it appears rather provincial and offers less shopping and dining possibilities.*

*There is a hotel in Momchilgrad that offers overnight accommodation. In the old hotel "Rodopi", time seems to have stood still. There are direct connections to Dimitrovgrad from the train station.*

## From Momcilgrad/Kardzhali to Ivajlovgrad    93 km

At the southern edge of town, turn left towards Krumovgrad in 33 kilometres' distance. Surrounded by the mountain range Stramni Rid, the route gradually leads uphill and soon you will have a beautiful view of the valley. After numerous curves you will reach the small town of **Zvezdel** and from there continue downhill to **Karamfil**. Directly after the curves, the white minaret of a small mosque can be seen. Then the road continues uphill again. You will have great views at the top before continuing downhill to **Gorna Kula**, where you will find a restaurant and a small store. This section is again exhausting but you will be rewarded by the beautiful landscape. Continue over the river Krumovica and through the valley to Krumovgrad.

## Krumovgrad

*The city was named after the medieval Bulgarian ruler Krum. The majority of the population is Turkish and the city has a well-kept centre with a large main square. The guesthouse "Enigma" and the three star hotel "VIA" offer good overnight accommodation.*

The road forks at the end of town. Turn left towards Ivajlovgrad. Continue uphill through **Pelin** which lies very idyllic between the mountains until you reach **Perunika**. This small vil-

lage also has a fantastic location. Fruit trees, meadows and houses built of stones dominate the picture. On little side roads, herds of sheep are brought to the fields and the clocks seem to turn more slowly here. The little village of **Chal** follows and near the road to Padalo you will again find a control station of the Bulgarian border police.

You will have a wide view over the hilly landscape, which often changes between fields and small oak woods. Shortly after a small chapel, you once again have a wonderful panoramic view.

At the fork in the road where you will find an obelisk, where the road makes a left towards Ljubimec and Svilengrad, a small spring invites you to take a break. Afterwards continue straight ahead to Ivajlovgrad.

## Ivajlovgrad

*It is fun to ride through the small streets of the somewhat hilly city with a population of 5,000. On the monumental square with the large stone memorial, a bronze plate was put up on a yellow building in commemoration of Georgi Dimitroff. The nearby surroundings are*

*Lake Ivajlovgrad*

*interesting. Apart from the reservoir named after the city, there are Thracian, Romanic, Byzantine and old Bulgarian legacies including the Roman villa "Armira" and the medieval fortification Ljutica. This belongs to the most well-maintained medieval fortresses in Bulgaria. The 1.75 metre thick walls are still maintained at their full height of six metres. The fortification is from the 12th/13th century but it is by no means the oldest: Previous discoveries date back as far as the 9th century. The road to the fortification leads over the still existing stone-arched bridge (Aterenski most) over the river Armira, a further*

point of interest in the region. You can spend the night in the hotel "Cemen" at the main square or in the hotel "Traker".

### From Ivajlovgrad (Bulgaria) to Petrotá (Greece)     75 km

From the centre of Ivajlovgrad, continue on the main road and turn right before the obelisk towards Ljubimec. Pass the fruit orchards and through a forest along a curvy road until you reach the dam at Lake Ivajlovgrad. On the other side you will come to a check point and have to stop at the barrier. For a while, continue along the northern shore of the lake and then to **Kamilski dol** along a curvy road. You have now travelled 23 kilometres from Ivajlovgrad and it is a further 40 kilometres before you reach the border crossing to Greece.

In the following town of **Dabovec** charcoal is still produced in a very traditional way. Large dark smoking heaps line both sides of the road that leads over a mountain to **Malko Gradiste**. Follow the yellow signs to the right towards Svilengrad.

Near the large river Marica, the surroundings are level so that you will soon reach the small town of **Siva Reka** with it's attractive church. You must deal with potholes for a short distance before you reach the railroad crossing that meets the E 80/85. Turn right towards Svilengrad. After two kilometres a blue sign points you to the right: it is a further three kilometres on the E 85 until you reach the border crossing between Bulgaria and Greece.

**Tip:** Note! You may not take any cheese, sausage or milk with you!

It is seven kilometres from the border crossing to the Greek town of Petrotá. Keep to the right and then straight ahead. Petrotá is also signposted. Between the vast fields and with a mountain range in sight, you will reach the town which looks very different to the Bulgarian towns.

## The history of Greece

Already in ancient times the area of today's Greece was the site of one of the most important antique cultures. The first larger ruled territories with centres developed and the Greeks began to expand in the Mediterranean area. The kingship was suppressed in most of the Greek States by an aristocracy and the community called "Polis" developed therefrom. The military regime Sparta and the Polis Athen advanced to become decisive rivals. The foundations of the antique democracy were developed in Athens through consecutive reforms. Under the leadership of Perikles, art, poetry and science flourished and are still an ideal of the occidental culture. Under the rule of Philipp II and his son Alexander the Great, Greece came under the control of Macedonia. Around 200 A.D. the Romans then took over from the Macedonians. This confirmed the end of the independence and the political supremacy of Greece.

Christianity established itself slowly. The area was under Byzantine rule from 330 A.D., belonged to the eastern part of the Empire and was split into alternating states. After taking over Constantinople in 1453, the Turks also conquered Greece, which then remained part of the Ottoman Empire until 1830. The country was ruled by Turkish Lords and only the church and the independent constitution of the communities kept the Greek nationalism alive during this period.

The collapse of the Ottoman Empire in the 17th and 19th century gave Greece the opportunity to battle for independence in the beginning of the 19th century. Secret societies played a major role in this. After the successful Serbian exaltation, the Greeks revolted against the Sultan. In 1821, the armed resistance began and one year later the National Assembly declared Greece as independent. It was the intervention of Great Britain, Russia and France, which made the foundation of the modern Greek state possible. It was a hereditary monarchy and comprised of large sections of today's national territory, whereby further areas were acquired during the Balkan Wars.

During World War I, Greece initially remained neutral. It then joined the war against the central powers and their allies - especially against Bulgaria and the Ottoman Empire - in 1917, after the allies had forced King Constantine I to resign.

After the war, Greece was able to claim large areas and Constantine I took over the throne again. The war against Turkey in Asia Minor however led to defeat. As a result, the Greeks living in Asia Minor were expelled and the border to Turkey was permanently defined. Attempts to replace the monarchy with a republic were unsuccessful and in 1936 a dictatorship was established.

During World War II, Greece was occupied by Italy, Germany and Bulgaria and its people were treated terribly. The end of World War II brought no end for Greece due to the outbreak of the Greek civil war between communists and royalist troops. Due to an agreement between the eastern and western powers, Greece was 90% influenced by Great Britain and only 10% by the Soviet Union. The communists were not able to assert themselves in Greece, unlike in its neighbouring countries. A new constitution was abolished, the monarchy remained and in 1952 Greece joined NATO. A new dark political phase followed when a group of conservative officers founded a dictatorial regime in 1967. The unsuccessful coup on Cyprus controlled from Athens led to the collapse of the military dictatorship in 1974. A new parliamentary de-

**Village square in Petrotá**

mocracy was established. Greece temporarily left NATO between 1974 and 1980. In 1981 it became part of the European Union.

## Petrotá

There is only little information about the remote area. Petrotá is qutie attractive with light, well kept buildings and gardens. At the central square with the light marble memorial, you will find two cafés and one store. You can spend the night in a private guest house.

Several residents speak a bit of German since there are numerous family connections to Germany, especially in the area of Ingol-

stadt where they were employed as migrant workers.

## From Petrotá (Greece) to Edirne (Turkey)    47 km

It is quite level towards the south to Pendálofos, later you will have a 10% uphill grade to conquer. The region is hilly and dominated by fields, grazing areas and individual groups of trees. In **Pendálofos** you will find a small white church and a small grocery store where you can stock up on food.

Keep to the right at the fork in the road at the end of town. Pass a large transmission pole and continue on the excellent pavement for eight kilometres with a great view until you reach **Komara**. Continue into the town with a 10% downhill grade and turn right over the Arda river until you reach Kyprinos in four kilometres. There is a hotel in the centre on the right side.

## Kyprinos

The majority of the Greek population has been in this area since the 1920's when a population exchange was agreed upon after the Greek-Turkish war. The peninsula seen

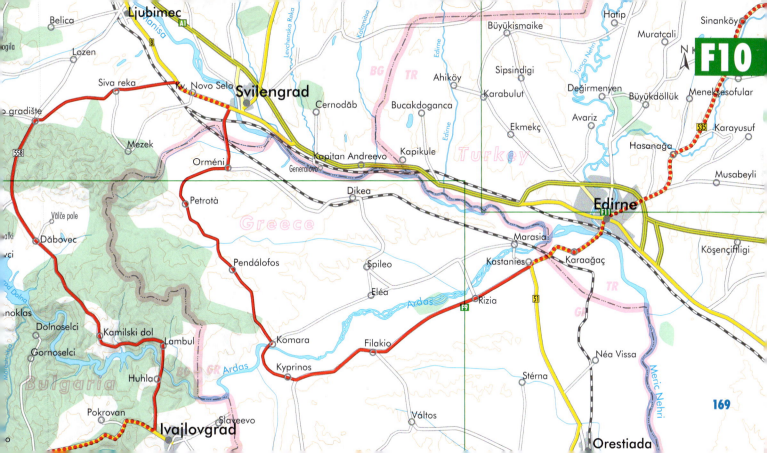

from Athens received electricity in the 1960's, television in the 1980's and also pavement. Nonetheless, the region especially suffered from the dramatic reduction of population in the last 20 years.

Keep to the left after Kyprinos towards Kastanies. Pass the vast cotton fields and you will reach the village of Filákio via Ammobouno with a large church worth visiting. At the small tavern on the corner, turn left towards Kastanies. Continue on the long road for eleven kilometres until you reach **Rízia**, which offers numerous shopping and dining possibilities. You can stroll along the main road. There is an attractive square in the centre.

It is five kilometres from here to the small town of Kastanies.

## Kastanies

This town is situated where the Arda merges into the Marica (Greek Evros) and has had to deal with numerous flooding disasters, one of the largest happened in 2005 and is still prevalent in the locals´ memories. Continue straight ahead to the border crossing into Turkey. If you expected heavy traffic here, you

Cotton fields

will be surprised: there is no sign of trucks. The sidewalk is painted blue to the white border line, afterwards red dominates. On both sides you will be observed by heavily armed but very friendly soldiers.

The Turks spend a lot of time checking your documents. In a building on a little roundabout, you will be sent through various rooms, where customs and border agents sit on old, heavy desks and control everything meticulously. Turkish flags hang everywhere and the founding father Atatürk is omnipresent on old portraits, paintings and posters.

"Hos Geldiniz" welcomes you to Turkey. Continue along the main road directly to Edirne. At a watermill continue over a stone bridge on a cobblestone road into the centre, which is five kilometres from the border crossing. It is best to orient yourself on the large mosque which you can see from afar.

Welcome to the Orient! The change from Bulgaria to Greece already seemed to be between two different worlds. But in Edirne you will be confronted with a completely different culture!

## The history of Turkey

The beginning of the Turkification and Islamification of today's Turkey was the sultanate of the Anatolic Seljuk which was formed in 1071 after the Seljuk sultan Alp Arslan's win over Byzantine. Many Turkish nomads moved to Asia Minor and the region subsequently prosper until the attack of the Mongols in 1243. Numerous small states formed the Ottoman Empire from the 14th century, which was named after the leader, Osman I. Ghasi, and began to expand towards the west. Thracia, Macedonia, Serbia,

Wallachia, Bulgaria and Thessaly gradually fell under Ottoman control. The last attempt to save the Byzantine Empire was prevented in 1444. At the end of the 15th century, the remaining Byzantine Empire was conquered and Constantinople became the new capital. The empire reached its peak in the 15th and 16th century with the conquering of additional areas in Europe, the Middle East and Northern Africa. It subsequently became an important political stakeholder and the leading sea power in the eastern Mediterranean. As of 1517, the Sultan also carried the title of Caliph and took over the protection of the holy sites of Islam in Mecca and Medina. Internally, Süleiman II created a central administration which remained in power for centuries.

In 1571, the defeat of the Ottoman fleet against the Holy League in the battle of Lepan was the beginning of the collapse. Regional rulers became more powerful and several uprisings weakened the government. Implemented reforms did not show the desired effect and the second occupation of Vienna in 1683 turned out to be a failure.

The following "Great Turkish War" with the Holy League brought great losses, the opponents of the empire became stronger and the Ottoman Empire lost a large part of the territory they had conquered in the beginning of the 20th century. World War I on the side of the central powers finally meant the end of the great power position of the Ottoman Empire.

The peace treaty of Sèvres (1920) dissolved the Ottoman Empire and reduced the Turkish territory to the area around Constantinople as well as parts of Asia Minor and Anatolia. The treaty signed by Sultan Mohammed VI and the existing government was not recognised by the commander and politician Mustafa Kemal Pascha, who later received the additional name Atatürk (Father of the Turks). As leader of the national party, he protested against the treaty, overthrew the government and formed the Turkish Republic with Angora (now Ankara) as the capital. His victory over the French, Italian and Greek army and the occupation of Turkey at the end of the war led to new

negotiations. The Treaty of Lausanne (1923) brought a more beneficial agreement for Turkey.

As president, Atatürk attempted to turn Turkey into a European-oriented secular nation. For this purpose, he introduced, among toher things, the Latin script. During World War II, the country was initially neutral but joined the Anti-Hitler coalition in 1945. During the Cold War, Turkey had a special role due to its western orientation. In 1952, it became the most eastern and only Muslim oriented member of NATO. In 1964 Turkey also requested to become a member of the European Union. The following governments continued the adaptation to the west, however there were also violent political interventions by the military. The occupation of the northern part of Cyprus by Turkish troops in 1974 caused national enthusiasm but also new conflicts with Greece and the western powers. A phase of inner instability was ended by a peaceful military coup in 1980. It was however followed by random arrests, executions and the pursuit of the Kurds living in Turkey. The Kurdish strive towards independence and the violent conflicts between the Kurdish PKK and the Turkish army still impact politics today.

In the 1990's, religious political movements became increasingly strong, but the pressure of the military prevented their stay in the government over a longer period of time. In 1999, the country achieved the status of a candidate country for the European Union and in March 2001, the government presented a "National Program" for the accssion procedure. In 2002, the winner of the political turbulences was the conservative Islamic AKP under the leadership of the former mayor of Istanbul, Recep Tayyip Erdogan. In the beginning, the new government implemented important reforms based on the EU accession procedure but afterwards significantly slowed down the speed of the reforms. In 2005, the acceptance negotiations with the EU were officially started. In the Iraq and Afghanistan War, Turkey was of enormous strategic importance as a NATO member due to its location and played a key role among the Islamic influenced countries. In 2007, the AKP was elected again with an absolute majority.

Edirne-Wall murals in the centre

The former Foreign Minister Abdullah Gül was elected as president. Resistance arose from the secular powers. In 2008 plans of a coup from a secret underground organisation named "Ergenekon" were discovered.

## Edirne

Edirne lies on the river Meriç Nehri (Bulgarian Marica, Greek Evros), which forms the border between Turkey and Greece and has a population of about 130,000. It is the capital of the province of the same name. it was (re) founded by the Roman Emperor as Hadrianopolis and was the site of 16 battles and occupations

since ancient Greece. During the alternating ownership between Bulgaria and Byzantine, it fell to the Ottomans in 1361 and even served as their capital until 1453. After a devastating fire in 1745, followed by a terrible earthquake six years later, the economic importance of the city was significantly reduced.

The oldest architectural structures are the remains of the Roman city wall. Especially interesting from modern times are the Selimiye Mosque from 1575 with the highest minaret in Turkey (70.9 m) and the Rüstem-Pasa-Karawanserei from 1554. Further older mosques and one of the oldest hospitals for psychiatric disorders (from 1488 (!), now a museum for psychiatric history) are also worth visiting.

There are numerous streets in the centre for shopping and three bazaars from the 15th and 16th century. Edirne also has numerous dining possibilities. Specialities are fried chicken livers, which are offered at most snack bars.

You can spend the night in the reasonably priced hotel "Sultan" on the Talatpasa Asfalti not far from the large mosque. In the breakfast

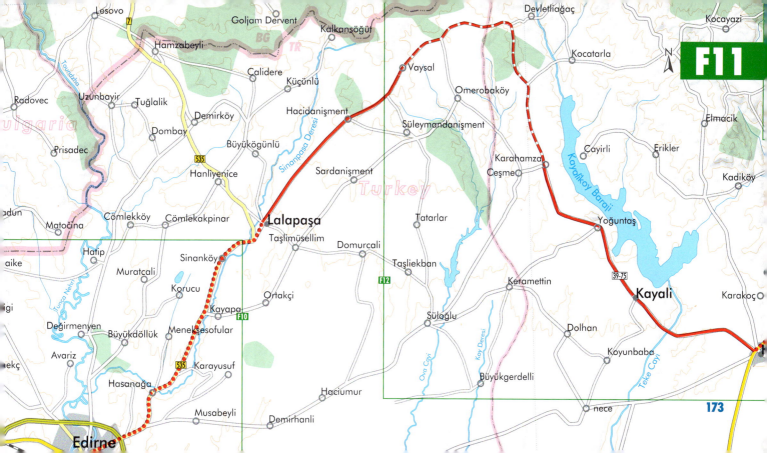

F11

173

*hall you can watch the news on a large television while enjoying cheese, bread and coffee. There are direct connections to Sofia from the train station.*

## Thracia

*Thracia once belonged to Greece. It now belongs to the eastern part of Turkey and forms the European part of the country. North Thracia belongs to Bulgaria and West Thracia to Greece.*

### From Edirne to Kırklareli     85 km

A very exciting section follows. Due to the difficult sign conditions in the Turkish province, this route does not apply with certainty. Taking all things into consideration, we tried to achiece a compromise. The target was to not only include main streets but instead more quiet roads.

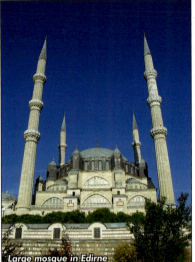
Large mosque in Edirne

In order to avoid the very remote and lonely appearing areas to the northeast of Vaysal, the route from Edirne leads you to Kırklareli over a northern stretch and from there directly to the border crossing to Bulgaria.

Pass the large mosque on the right along the main road to Lalapasa. The destinations are luckily signposted here, which is unfortunately not the case in small towns and on side roads. On the new and little travelled road, the 21 kilometres are soon conquered. Before you turn right on the bumpy pavement to Lalapasa, you have a 10 % downhill grade to look forward to. In **Lalapasa** you will find a large mosque with two minarets and several stores.

Continue to the northeast. The road leads through a very lonely area which looks like the surface of the moon when it is foggy. Sheep seek for the scarce grass between the pointy piles of stones and thorny bushes. This landscape appears endless. At a curve, you can finally get a view of the larger town of **Hacidanişment**, from which a minaret reaches toward the sky. In this town, which does not have a sign, the streets are sandy and bumpy. Pass the mosque and numerous houses which line the valley.

Afterwards, a new but very coarse paved road leads to **Vaysal** whereby you must overcome a slight hill. If necessary, you can ask the locals for the name of the town since there are no signs here either and unfortunately also no pavement. Gradually the road becomes overgrown. High bushes grow on both sides. On the left, red signs warn you not to enter the military zone, since you are now close to the Bulgarian border. At the fork in the road about ten kilometres after Vaysal, turn right to the south towards Kirklareli.

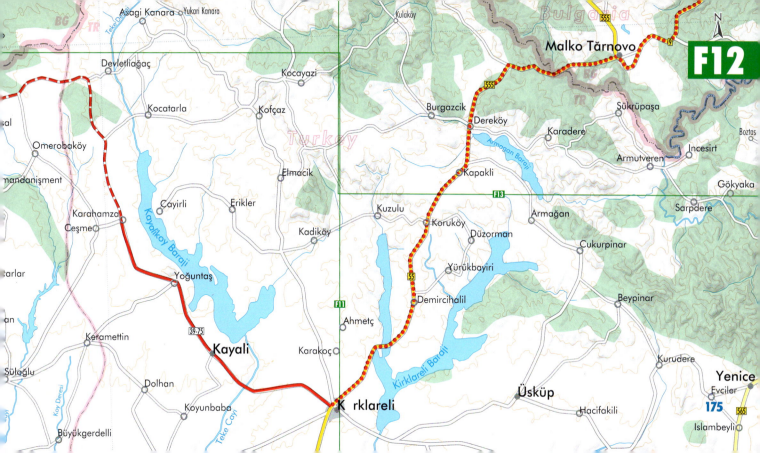

## Karahamza

In Karahamza, which you will reach after having cycled past oak woods, meadows and fields, it will feel like you have joint civilisation again.

On the way to Yoğuntaş the road conditions will gradually improve.

## Yoğuntaş

On the main square in the centre of town, there is an impressive mosque as well as two stores and a community centre, where you can drink tea with the locals. Most of them only speak Turkish, but they normally do their best to help. If you approach them in a friendly way, you will quickly find yourself invited to tea and half of the village coming to see you!

There is also a small store in **Kayalı** at the mosque, where you can purchase any necessities. At the end of town, interesting cliff formations can be found. The road continues through the meadows, which alternate with cliffs and rocks. You should take your time and enjoy the beautiful landscape even though the hilly section can be exhausting in high temperatures.

*Before Kırklareli*

In the small town of **Erelice** you should pay attention to the wild dogs. A little later you will reach Kırklareli, which greets you with high-rise buildings.

## Kırklareli

*The capital of the region with the same name lies at an elevation of 203 metres and has a population of about 79,000. The Byzantine-Greek name is "Forty Candles", which the Ottomans translated into "Kırk Kilise".*

*Already in around 5,000 B. C., the first settlements of the Bronze Age existed here. The complex Hızır bey is worth visiting: The mosque from* 1383 with a single minaret, the bath house of the same time, which is still in operation, and the bazaar with its interesting arch construction. Kırklareli does not have much tourism and it is somewhat difficult for foreigners to find their way around.

You can spend the night in the "Yaman" hotel in the centre. It is considered a hostel and a double room costs between € 25 and 30, depending on the season.

### From Kırklareli (Turkey) to Malko Tarnovo (Bulgaria)    50 km

Follow the signs from Kırklareli towards "Bulgaristan" and Derekoy. The route is not complicated. Follow the E 87 for 40 kilometres to the Turkish-Bulgarian border. The road is wide, well constructed and little travelled. Since there are no trees, the road surface can become very hot in the summer, which makes this hilly section very exhausting.

After several kilometres, the road becomes narrower and you will reach the village of **Koruköy**. Continue uphill through small oak and pine woods until you reach **Kapaklı** and

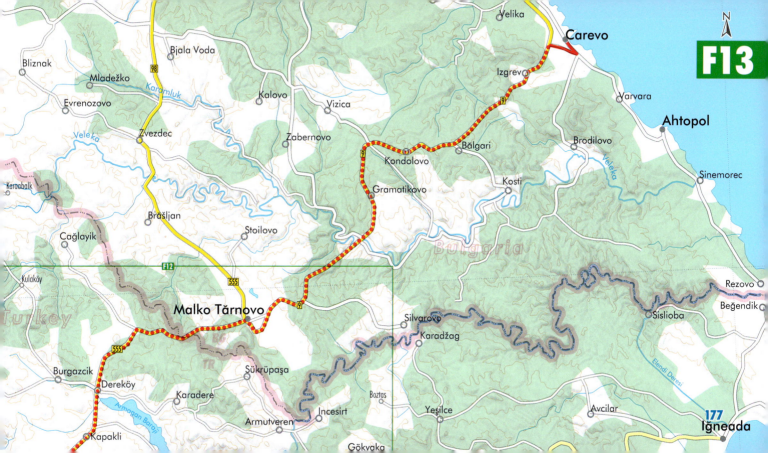

Shortly before the border to Bulgaria

## Malko Tarnovo

*Nearly 3,000 people live in Malko Tarnovo, which appears rather small. A small stream flows through the centre and is lined by old wooden and stone houses, which invite you to take a closer look. Apart from excavation sites, the city also has a historic museum. Christianity dominates here and you will find Orthodox and Catholic churches and chapels. You will also find various eateries and overnight accommodation here.*

The river Veleka by Malko Tarnovo

afterwards further downhill. Cross a river and continue through the valley.

It is about twelve kilometres from the small village of **Derekoy** to the border. The landscape changes abruptly. Continue through deciduous forests and you will feel like you are in Germany. One last hill remains before you reach the border crossing. It is bigger and more travelled than the border between Greece and Turkey at Edirne and you must wait in a linequeue. You still have ten kilometres of windy road ahead of you until you reach the small Bulgarian city of Malko Tarnovo.

### From Malko Tarnovo to Carevo          55 km

**Follow the signs on the last stretch to Carevo. The pavement is overall in good condition over the entire stretch. However, there still are a few cracks and potholes and you should be careful when travelling downhill!**

First you will travel mostly downhill through a wooded area until you reach the Veleka river. There you will have very sharp curves to steer through! Continue over a long bridge and after the river uphill with a ten percent grade. At the top you will reach the small

village of **Gramatikovo**, where the wooded area opens up.

The road conditions are rather poor in the very lonely and old village of **Kondolovo**. You will however be rewarded with the beautiful landscape and you will have a wide view over the hilly region.

At the branch to Kosti, you will again be confronted with a control post of the Bulgarian border police and you will have to produce your papers once again. Continue downhill from here. Soon you will get your first glimpse of the Black Sea.

Carevo lies in an idyllic bay and has a romantic harbour. There you should end your tour. Continue straight ahead through the city to the shore and look out over the waves of the ocean and the fishing and sports boats. The final destination of a tour could not be nicer.

## Carevo

In this protected bay the water warms up more quickly than at other locations on the Bulgarian shores of the Black Sea. This is why Carevo, with a population of 6,000, is so popular among the Bulgarians. The area is also not overrun by international tourists and is therefore rather quiet.

The city became known in the 12th century as Vasiliko. It was on the southern edge of the bay where the district of the same name lies. After a devastating fire in 1882, it was rebuilt on the northern edge. Tsar Boris III from Bulgaria encouraged the development of the city so that it was renamed Carevo out of thankfulness to him (Vasiliko was derived from the Byzantine Emperor title Basileus). From 1950 to 1991, it was named after the Soviet botanist Muchurin.

On the Papia mountain with an elevation of 502 metres, you will find the ruins of an old fortification. The old churches and the renovated cultural house on the central square are interesting sights to visit.

Carevo has a goog choice of overnight accommodation in private houses, guest houses and hotels. For example, the hotel "Tzarevo Plaza" in the Asparuch has a view of the ocean. The hotel "Tschaika" is directly next to a stone memorial in a small park. A good tip to indulge your culinary senses is the "Mechana Gorski Kat" in the Vasil Levski.

**Black Sea in Carevo**

## Departure towards home:

You can depart for Germany from the northern coastal cities of Varna or Burgas. It is about 65 kilometres to Burgas and twice as far to Varna. It is easiest to take a car to Burgas. Numerous airlines depart from there to Germany as well as from Varna.

# Index of places

Page numbers in *green* refer to the list of accommodations.